Walk, Amble, Stroll

Vocabulary Building Through Domains
Level 1

Kathryn Trump
Sherry Trechter
Dee Ann Holisky

All of George Mason University

 Heinle & Heinle Publishers
A Division of International Thomson Publishing, Inc.
Boston, Massachusetts 02116 U.S.A.

Pacific Grove • Albany • Bonn • Boston • Cincinnati • Detroit • London • Madrid • Melborne
Mexico City • New York • Paris • San Francisco • Tokyo • Toronto • Washington

Heinle & Heinle Publishers
20 Park Plaza
Boston, MA 02116 U.S.A

International Thomson Publishing
Berkshire House 168-173
High Holbern
London WC1V7AA
England

Thomas Nelson Australia
102 Dodds Street
South Melbourne, 3205
Victoria, Australia

Nelson Canada
1120 Birchmont Road
Scarborough, Ontario
Canada M1K5G4

International Thomson Publishing
  Gmbh
Königwinterer Strasse 418
53227 Bonn
Germany

International Thomson Publishing Asia
Block 211 Henderson Road
  #08-03
Henderson Industrial Park
Singapore 0315

International Thomson Publishing-
  Japan
Hirakawacho-cho Kyowa
  Building, 3F
2-2-1 Hirakawacho-cho
Chiyoda-ku, 102 Tokyo
Japan

The publication of *Walk, Amble, Stroll, Level One,* was directed by members of the Newbury House Publishing Team at Heinle & Heinle

Elizabeth Holthaus, Team Leader
Erik Gundersen, Editorial Director
John McHugh, College ESL/EFL Market Development Director
Martha Leibs, Production Editor

Also participating in the publication of this program were:
Publisher: **Stanley J. Galek**
Director of Production: **Elizabeth Holthaus**
Project Manager: **Judy Keith**
Assistant Editor: **Karen P. Hazar**
Promotions and Advertising Manager: **Elaine Leary**
Associate Production Editor: **Maryellen Eschmann**
Manufacturing Coordinator: **Mary Beth Hennebury**
Illustrator: **Bob Doucet**
Interior Design: **Susan Gerould/Perspectives**
Cover Illustration: *Pertaining to Nassau Street, New York, 1936* by
  John Marin. Collection of the Sheldon Memorial Art Gallery,
  University of Nebraska-Lincoln
Cover Designer: **Hannus Design Associates**

Manufactured in the United States of America

ISBN 0-8384-3956-X

10   9   8   7   6   5   4   3   2   1

▶ DEDICATIONS

To my mother, who taught me to care about language. *(D.H.)*

To George Mason University ELI students everywhere. *(S.T.)*

To Scott Alan Trump. *(K.T.)*

▶ ACKNOWLEDGMENTS

We would like to acknowledge all the colleagues, family, and friends who helped us write this book by encouraging us, listening to us, suggesting changes, giving us new ideas, piloting chapters, or giving us space when we needed it.

We are also appreciative of the many good ideas given to us by those who reviewed early versions of the manuscript:

Christopher M. Ely, Ball State University

Julie Falsetti, Hunter College

Kathi Jordan, Contra Costa College

Ellen Koch, Suffolk Community College

Ellen Mintz, Oakland Community College

Finally, we want to say thank you to Karen Hazar and Erik Gundersen at Heinle & Heinle, as well as to Judy Keith, Project Manager, and Lois Poulin and Carol Shanahan for their careful and caring attention to all the details that went into the production of the book.

▶ Contents

▶ TO THE STUDENT

The idea for *Walk, Amble, Stroll: Levels One and Two* started with an ESL teacher. She wanted to help her students learn a lot of new words quickly and easily. She taught her students different words for the basic word *walk*. The students learned the words quickly, remembered them, and had fun, too. The teacher and the students were happy. The teacher began to teach more and more words this way. That's how *Walk, Amble, Stroll* began.

Each chapter in this book has one or more domains. A domain is a group of words that are related to one basic idea. For example, in the EAT domain, you will learn many words and expressions that mean *to eat*, such as *pick at, nibble on, lick,* and *pig out*. These words add extra meaning to the basic idea of *eat*.

Word domains will help you learn many new words. You will learn to attach many new words to one basic word that you already know.

Learning new vocabulary is an important way to improve your English. We hope this book will help you. We also hope you will have some fun with the words.

Dee Holisky

Sherry Trechter

Kathy Trump

▶ TO THE TEACHER

Walk, Amble, Stroll: Vocabulary Building Through Domains is a textbook for English as a second or foreign language (ESL/EFL) students at the high beginning level who are ready to expand their vocabulary. It can be used in a class devoted to vocabulary building or as a supplementary text in a reading, writing, or integrated skills class. It can also be used for self-study by individual students. (An Answer Key is available in the Instructor's Manual.)

Rapid and continual vocabulary expansion is critical for ESL/EFL students. Our goal in writing this book is to provide students with an efficient and enjoyable way to expand their vocabulary. We introduce vocabulary through a concept and teach words that are related to that concept. We call this group of related words a *domain*. The focus on concepts and word domains lends itself to a rich variety of activities that appeals to students with different learning styles.

Major Features of This Book

1. The words to be taught are presented in a domain, a group of related words. It is well known that learning is facilitated when new material is structured in some way. Word domains provide this structure, and students learn a larger number of words more quickly.

2. The target vocabulary is displayed in a chart in which the positioning of the words reflects certain aspects of their relationship to one another. This aids students in visualizing the domains and in remembering the words.

3. The words are used in a variety of context-rich sentences and paragraphs.

4. The words are reinforced by a developmental progression of exercises, from simple manipulation, to problem solving, to more complex and open-ended activities. Students move gradually from beginning practice with the words into creating their own contexts for using them.

5. As students begin to understand the concept of word domains, they learn a new way to learn vocabulary. Teachers can take advantage of the domain concept to teach other words as they come up in the classroom.

Format of *Walk, Amble, Stroll*

This book consists of four units. Each unit contains three chapters related to a common theme. Within each chapter there are several vocabulary domains. The presentation of each domain follows a similar format.

1. **Getting Ready.** The first section of each domain consists of a few questions to help the student focus on the concept behind the domain and to introduce the need for the new words. Though it might be tempting to skip this section if time is short, it is important to spend some time preparing the students to be receptive to the new vocabulary.

2. **The Domain.** The second section presents the target vocabulary in a domain chart. The placement of words on the chart reflects aspects of the structure of the domain. Wherever possible, the domain chart has illustrations to clarify the meanings of words.

   It is important to spend some time examining the domain chart with your students. You can briefly discuss the words in the domain, its organization, the placement of words, and the illustrations.

   Some students will already know some of the words in the domain. They may want to volunteer information about the meanings of these words. All students should have a basic grasp of the domain before they go on.

   Students should be encouraged to refer back to the domain chart as they do the exercises that follow. Sometimes they can do the exercise while looking at the domain chart; at other times they can study the chart and then try to do the exercise without looking. For many of the written exercises, they can use the domain chart to check their answers.

3. **Exploring the Domain.** This section consists of a short reading in which the words are used in context. The target vocabulary is shown in boldface type so the student can easily identify it. There is usually a major illustration to accompany the reading. The illustration clarifies the content of the reading and provides a visual for further discussions.

4. **Exercises**. Once students have been introduced to the vocabulary and seen it used in context, they are ready for some active practice. The exercises in *Walk, Amble, Stroll* follow a progression that gives them practice in using the words in a variety of ways. It is important to do at least some exercises from each of the three steps in this progression.

   a. **Manipulation of the new words.** The first step involves manipulative exercises that familiarize the students with the words and the basic dimensions of the domain. In these beginning exercises, students hear, pronounce, and write the new words. The focus is on their oral and written forms.

These types of activities help put new words in short-term memory. Though they may at times seem "simple" or "low-level," the purpose is to familiarize students with the forms of the new words before they are asked to do anything more complex.

b. Problem-solving using the new words. Exercises of the second type go beyond the simple focus on form. They are problem-solving activities that require students to demonstrate an understanding of the meaning of the words in context. Common examples of this type of activity require students to choose the best word to complete a particular sentence or to characterize a particular situation. "Sense-Nonsense" exercises require students to determine whether a sentence using a new word makes sense or is nonsense.

Research has shown that exercises of this type involve a deeper level of processing. They help put the new vocabulary in long-term memory.

c. Open-ended use of the new words. Exercises of the third type require students to perform tasks that use the vocabulary, but don't focus on it. For example, for every domain there are exercises "For Writing or Discussion." These exercises generate discussion on topics that encourage use of the new vocabulary.

These exercises can be used in a variety of ways, depending on time, the level of the students, the size of the class, and the preferences of the teacher. The questions can be discussed orally with the class as a whole, in small groups, or in pairs. They can be used as a writing assignment done alone or in pairs. The writing can be shared with the whole class or a small group.

For each domain we have tried to provide a range of questions that will appeal to different learners. Students can choose to answer questions they are most interested in.

An Answer Key for all the exercises is included in the Instructor's Manual.

Other Information for Using This Book

1. Order of Presentation. The units in this book do not have to be covered in order. However, we have used vocabulary taught in earlier chapters in the readings and exercises of later chapters. Also, the chapters become progressively more difficult as one proceeds through the book.

2. **Teaching Speed.** Students using this book tend to learn words more quickly than they do using other vocabulary materials. It has been our experience that because the vocabulary is organized around a familiar concept, teachers can move through the chapters more quickly than usual.

3. **Instructor's Manual.** The separate Instructor's Manual that accompanies this text contains the Answer Key as well as Unit Reviews that systematically review all the words from the units. Each Unit Review contains a crossword puzzle and other exercises to review the words, as well as a reading passage that incorporates words from all the domains in the unit. A whole class activity is included in most Unit Reviews.

4. **Using Dictionaries.** There are no definitions provided for the vocabulary taught in this book. Knowing the dictionary definition of a word does not necessarily help a student understand what the word means or use it appropriately. Most students can effectively learn the meanings of the new words in this book through their placement on the domain chart, through the illustrations provided, and by their use in context, particularly in the narratives in "Exploring the Domain."

Some students want a written definition, however. In some cases a bilingual dictionary or an English-English dictionary may help clarify the meaning of a word for the student, and, thus, we do not discourage the use of dictionaries of either type.

5. **Other Activities.** The exercises we have designed should serve only as a starting point for working with vocabulary. We hope that you will expand on the exercises in this book by creating games and other activities for manipulating the new words and by constructing related reading and writing assignments for content-oriented use of the words. We also hope you will encourage your students to expand the domains you are teaching by bringing in examples of words from the domains that they have encountered in their everyday lives.

It has been exciting for us to see other teachers use these materials and design their own activities. The resources cited on the next page may give you some further ideas. Be as creative, original, innovative, inventive, imaginative, and ingenious as you can.

Resources for the Teacher

Aitchison, Jean. *Words in the Mind: An Introduction to the Mental Lexicon*. Oxford: Basil Blackwell. 1987

Gairns, Ruth and Stuart Redman. *Working with Words, A Guide to Teaching and Learning Vocabulary*. Cambridge: Cambridge University Press. 1986

McCarthy, Michael. *Vocabulary*. Oxford: Oxford University Press. 1990

Nagy, William. *Teaching Vocabulary to Improve Reading Comprehension*. Urbana, Illinois: National Council of Teachers of English. 1988.

Nation, I.S.P. *Teaching and Learning Vocabulary*. Boston, Massachusetts: Heinle & Heinle. 1990.

Nation, Paul, Editor. *New Ways in Teaching Vocabulary*. Alexandria, Virginia: Teachers of English to Speakers of other Languages, Inc. 1994.

Trump, Kathyrn, Sherry Trechter and Dee Ann Holisky. *Walk, Amble, Stroll, Level 2*. Boston, Massachusetts: Heinle & Heinle, 1992

Walk,
Amble,
Stroll

1

It's About Time!

This unit is about *time*. Time is important to most people. We measure it in many ways. We talk about it using many different words.

CHAPTER 1
From Seconds to Centuries

GETTING READY Domain 1

1. Do you wear a watch? Do most people in your country wear a watch? How often do you look at your watch?

2. A clock has two hands. What does the big hand measure? What does the little hand measure?

3. The words below are used to measure time. Work with a partner. Put the words in order from the shortest time to the longest time. Do as many as you can. Don't use a dictionary. Then look at the next page to check your answers.

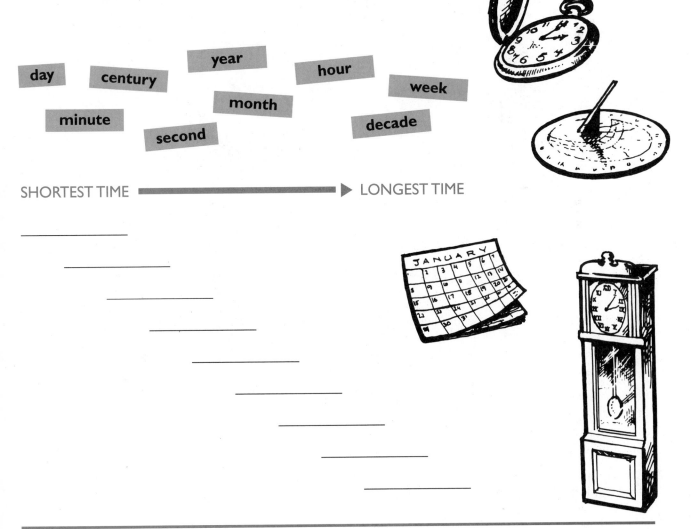

day   century   year   hour

minute   month   week

second   decade

SHORTEST TIME ━━━━━━━▶ LONGEST TIME

_____

_____

_____

_____

_____

_____

_____

_____

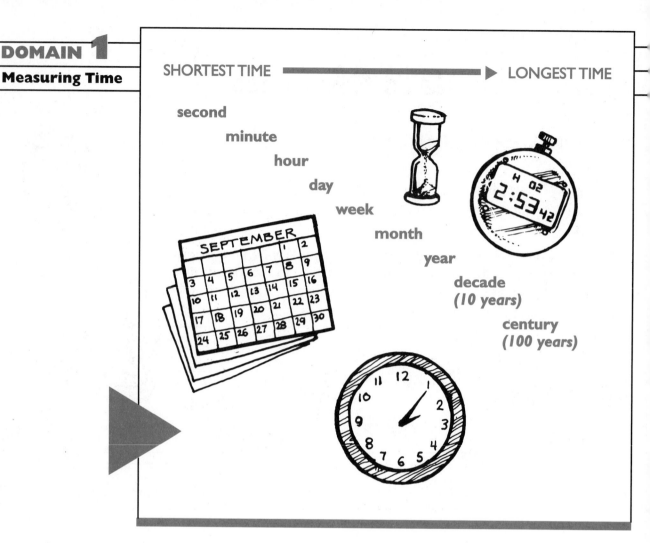

SHORTEST TIME ➡ LONGEST TIME

second
minute
hour
day
week
month
year
decade
(10 years)
century
(100 years)

EXPLORING THE DOMAIN

In the past, communication was slow. In 1950, business papers were sent by mail. A letter from the United States arrived in Thailand after three **weeks** or even a **month**. Telephone calls to other countries were not easy. Usually, the caller waited several **hours** or even a **day**. The operator connected the call when a line was available.

Now, four **decades** later, we can communicate with someone on the other side of the world in **seconds**. We can use telephones, fax machines, or computers to send messages very quickly. In less than a **minute**, a Brazilian company can fax a contract to an office in Germany.

How fast do you think communication will be in the **year** 2001? How fast do you think it will be in the next **century**?

Exercise 1 *Beginning Practice*

Put the words in order from shortest time to longest time.

1. minute, hour, second _____, _____, _____

2. month, week, day _____, _____, _____

3. year, century, decade _____, _____, _____

4. month, minute, decade _____, _____, _____

5. hour, century, second _____, _____, _____

6. week, year, day _____, _____, _____

Exercise 2 *Speaking Practice*

Work with a partner. Your partner says a word from the domain and then says "longer" or "shorter." You give a correct word from the domain. Take turns.

Example: Your partner says: "year - longer"
                    You say: "decade" OR "century"

Exercise 3 *Matching*

Match two words with each number or group of numbers. Then create a sentence for each pair of words. (Be careful. Sometimes you will need a plural form of a word.)

Example: 7 _____*days*_____ _____*week*_____

You say or write: "There are seven days in a week."

1. 12 _____ _____

2. 60 _____ _____

3. 10 _____ _____

4. 100 _____ _____

5. 7 _____ _____

6. 52 _____ _____

second	day
week	minute
month	year
hour	century
decade	

7. 365 _____ _____

8. 24 _____ _____

9. 4 to 4 1/2 _____ _____

10. 28, 29, 30 or 31 _____ _____

Exercise 4 *Word Choice*

In English we use the verb *take* to talk about time.
(The past tense of *take* is *took*.)

It **takes** many months to learn English.

It **took** five hours to drive to Atlanta yesterday.

It **takes** me five minutes to walk to work.

A. Complete each sentence with an appropriate word for measuring time.

1. How long does it take to build a new house?

It takes about six _____.

2. How long did it take to build the space shuttle?

It took many _____.

3. How long does it take you to run a mile?

It takes me about _____.

4. How long did it take Yukako to finish her homework?

It took her three _____.

5. How long does it take to cook an egg?

It takes about _____.

6. How long does it take to change a rock to sand?

It takes _____.

B. Now create some questions and answers of your own. Some of the sentences are in the present tense and some are in the past.

1. How long does it take to _____?

   It takes _____

2. How long does it take to _____?

   It takes _____

3. How long did it take to _____?

   It took _____

4. How long did it take to _____?

   It took _____

Exercise 5 *For Discussion or Writing*

Your teacher may ask you to answer these questions individually, with a partner, or in a small group.

1. What was the best year of your life? Why?

2. Which decade has the best popular music—the 60s, 70s, 80s, or 90s? Why?

3. Choose one century—the eighteenth, nineteenth, or twentieth century. Describe one important event that happened in your country in that century.

4. What was the best century in human history? Why?

GETTING READY Domain 2

1. What is your favorite time of the day? Why?

2. Where is the sun in the morning? At noon? At night?

3. The words below name parts of the day. Work with a partner. Put
the words in order from the beginning of the day to the end. Do as
many as you can. Don't use a dictionary. Then look at the next page
to check your answers.

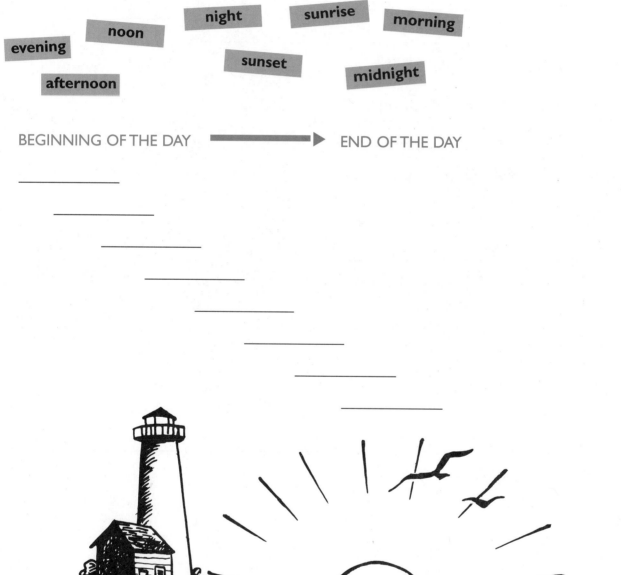

night   sunrise   morning

noon

evening   sunset

afternoon   midnight

BEGINNING OF THE DAY ⟶ END OF THE DAY

_____

_____

_____

_____

_____

_____

_____

_____

PARTS OF THE DAY

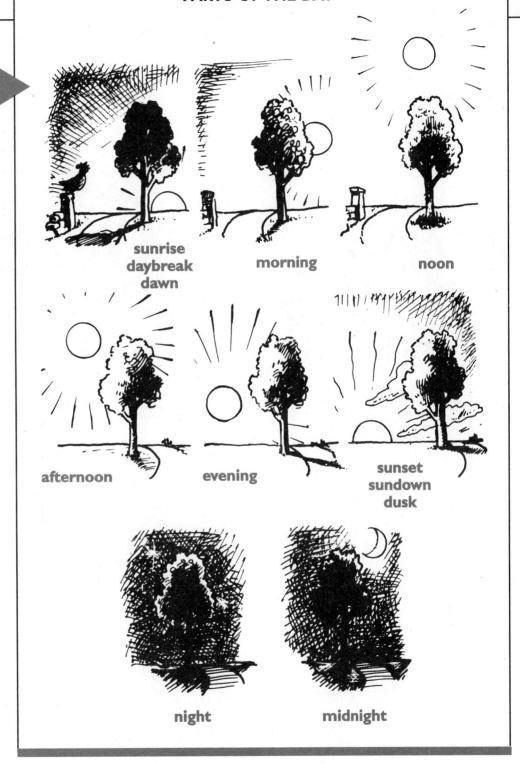

sunrise
daybreak
dawn

morning

noon

afternoon

evening

sunset
sundown
dusk

night

midnight

EXPLORING THE DOMAIN

For some people, the day begins at **dawn**. These people are early birds. They like to get up at **sunrise**. They do their best work in the **morning**. By **noon**, they have finished most of their work. They like to go to bed early.

Other people are night owls. They like to get up at noon. When the sun goes down, they don't think about going to bed. At **sunset** they still have many hours to work or play. Some of them do their best work in the **evening**. They like to stay up late at **night**. They don't go to bed before **midnight**. How about you? Are you a night owl or an early bird?

Dawn and **dusk** come at different times in different seasons of the year. For example, in Alaska in the summer, **sundown** comes at 2:00 or 3:00 A.M. But in the winter it comes in the middle of the **afternoon.** When does the sun rise and set in your country in the winter and in the summer?

Exercise 6 *Beginning Practice*

Put the words in order from the beginning of the day to the end of the day.

1. night   morning   noon

_____ _____ _____

2. afternoon   daybreak   dusk

_____ _____ _____

3. midnight   dawn   twilight

_____ _____ _____

4. morning   night   evening

_____ _____ _____

Exercise 7 *Speaking Practice*

Work with a partner. You cover the domain. Your partner says a word from the domain and then says "before" or "after." You give a correct word from the domain. Take turns.

Example: Your partner says: "sundown; after"
                  You say: "night" OR "midnight"

Exercise 8 *Speaking Practice*

A. Work with a partner. You ask a question about a part of the day. Your partner then answers it.

Example: **You say:** "What do you usually do at noon?"
       Your partner says: "At noon I usually eat lunch."

1. at noon   **3.** in the evening   **5.** in the afternoon

2. in the morning   **4.** at night

B. Now your partner asks the questions and you answer.

Example: Your partner says: "When do you eat lunch?"
                 You say: "I eat lunch at noon."

1. eat dinner   **3.** watch the sun come up   **5.** watch television

2. go to bed   **4.** do your homework   **6.** play soccer

Exercise 9 *Word Find*

Find the following words in the letter box. The words can be horizontal →
or vertical ↓. *Midnight* has been done for you.

```
v  a  f  t  e  r  n  o  o  n  h  o  p  p
e  r  q  u  m  c  s  e  p  t  k  w  t  t
t  a  l  j  m  s  s  g  i  s  e  l  r  d
p  a  c  n  i  e  w  h  d  u  o  p  e  a
r  e  a  n  d  r  q  x  m  n  y  r  a  w
n  r  t  s  n  c  m  l  o  r  e  n  n  n
o  i  t  r  i  t  l  s  n  i  o  n  r  r
p  r  g  v  g  w  t  d  f  s  i  o  e  x
e  t  r  h  h  t  y  u  n  e  o  o  v  z
m  e  f  j  t  o  d  w  e  t  n  n  e  e
o  o  p  b  g  c  e  n  t  u  r  y  n  j
r  i  l  m  n  o  c  l  o  c  t  n  i  i
n  r  t  b  o  l  a  d  s  w  r  a  n  w
i  t  e  d  x  m  d  r  o  i  g  r  g  g
n  p  e  g  s  l  e  q  u  o  l  s  f  f
g  l  o  r  u  u  y  o  p  d  u  s  k  k
p  n  i  g  h  t  n  r  s  f  c  z  o  a
q  n  m  o  p  d  s  s  a  c  l  k  o  q
```

midnight
afternoon
night
dawn
noon
dusk
sunrise
morning
evening
century
decade
twilight

Exercise 10 *For Discussion or Writing*

Answer the following questions. Your teacher may ask you to do this exercise in writing or orally (in a small group or with a partner).

1. What is your favorite part of the day? Why do you like this part of
   the day best?

2. When do you have the most energy, in the morning or in the afternoon?

3. Do you like to stay up late at night? What do you do?

4. What are you usually doing at sundown in the summer? In the winter?

5. Some people have to get up at dawn to go to work. What kind of
   job do they have? Do you want a job like that?

CHAPTER 2
Then and Now

GETTING READY Domain 1

1. What were you doing yesterday at 10:00 A.M.?

2. What are you doing now?

3. What will you do tomorrow at 6:00 P.M.?

Study the domain below for a few minutes.

DOMAIN 1

Yesterday, Today,

Tomorrow

PAST	PRESENT	FUTURE
yesterday	today	tomorrow
yesterday morning	this morning	tomorrow morning
yesterday afternoon	this afternoon	tomorrow afternoon
yesterday evening	this evening	tomorrow evening
last night	tonight	tomorrow night

the day before yesterday   the day after tomorrow

last week	this week	next week
last month	this month	next month
last year	this year	next year

EXPLORING THE DOMAIN

(The calendar that follows the reading passage will help you understand the new words.)

Wen is a student at Wisconsin State University. This is his last year at the university. He is a senior. Wen has a job in the university bookstore.

Today is Tuesday, March 15. **This morning** he will work in the bookstore from 9:00 to 11:00 A.M. **Tonight** he will study for a biology test.

Yesterday Wen was very busy. He had a job interview **yesterday afternoon** at 2:00 P.M. **Last night** he went to the library to study.

The day before yesterday Wen went to a movie with Christina. They have been good friends since they met at Wisconsin State University three years ago.

Tomorrow morning he has a biology test. **Tomorrow afternoon**, after the test, he is going to go to a meeting of the International Club. He will see many of his friends there.

The day after tomorrow he has to go to traffic court because he got a speeding ticket. He was driving 40 miles an hour on a city street. He hopes he will not have to pay a big fine.

This week is a busy week for Wen. He has many activities on his schedule. But **next week** he is free. He is going to go to the beach with some friends. He hopes to relax and have some fun there.

Week of March 13–19							
	SUNDAY MARCH 13	MONDAY MARCH 14	TUESDAY MARCH 15	WEDNESDAY MARCH 16	THURSDAY MARCH 17	FRIDAY MARCH 18	SATURDAY MARCH 19
8:00					8:30 COURT		
9:00			↑work	*TEST biology		↑work	
10:00			↓			↓	
11:00							Shopping
12:00							
1:00	↑						
2:00	work	*JOB INTERVIEW					
3:00	↓			Internat'l			
4:00				Club			
5:00							
6:00							
7:00	7:30	↑Library		7:30			
8:00	movie —	↓	↑study for test	meeting		Basketball game	
9:00	Student Center		↓				
10:00							
11:00							

Exercise 1 *Beginning Practice*

Work with a partner. Imagine that today is Thursday, March 17. Use Wen's calendar to talk about what Wen did, is doing, or will do at the times given below.

Example: **You see:** yesterday morning
You say: "Yesterday morning Wen had a biology test."

1. tomorrow night
2. the day after tomorrow
3. yesterday afternoon

4. last night
5. the day before yesterday
6. this morning

Exercise 2 *More Beginning Practice*

Complete each series of words.

PAST ➡ PRESENT ➡ FUTURE

1. last month   _____   next month

2. _____   this evening   tomorrow evening

3. last night   tonight   _____

4. _____   this afternoon   tomorrow afternoon

Exercise 3 *Word Choice*

Put a phrase from the domain in each blank.

1. Robin is a student at law school. ___Last year___ he begun his studies. _____ he is a second-year student. _____ he will graduate.

2. It is exam week at Wisconsin State University. Jon has five exams. _____ he studied for his exams. He is taking his exams _____. He will be on vacation _____.

3. Eugenia is a salesperson. She sells watches. She receives a bonus (extra money) each month if she sells a lot of watches. Today is June 13. She will get a $60 bonus at the end of _____. She received an $85 bonus _____. She doesn't know how much she will get _____.

Month	Bonus
May	$85
June	$60
July	?

4. Ted has many things to do this week. He's busy every night. He went to a movie from 8:00-11:00 P.M. _____. He is going to a meeting at 7:30 P.M. _____. He is going on a date with Sara _____.

Exercise 4 *Speaking Practice*

Work with a partner. You cover the domain. Your partner says a word from the domain and you tell what you were doing or will do at that time. Take turns.

Example: **Your partner says:** "tomorrow evening"
You say: "Tomorrow evening I will watch television."

Exercise 5 *Speaking Practice*

Work with a partner. Imagine that it is Wednesday at 10:00 A.M. You are in your sociology class. Your professor is assigning a project. You must do this project with your partner. You have to find a time when you and your partner can meet for two hours to work on the project.

First, fill in the schedule below. Write in the times when you are in class, working, studying, etc. Then talk to your partner. Find a time when you and your partner can work together on the project

Start your conversation with: "Are you free tomorrow at 9 A.M.?"

OR: "Are you busy tomorrow morning at 9 A.M.?"

Do not look at your partner's schedule.

	Wednesday	Thursday	Friday	Monday
Morning	Sociology Class			
Afternoon				
Evening				

GETTING READY Domain 2

1. Tell about something that happened in the eighteenth century (1700s).

2. Tell about something that happened last month.

3. Tell about something that is happening in the world right now.

Look over the domain below. Then read the passage.

DOMAIN 2

The Past

and Present

THE PAST AND PRESENT		
PAST	RECENT PAST	PRESENT
a long time ago	a short time ago	now
at one time	recently	right now
some time ago		at this moment
	*the other day	at this point
		at this time
*ages ago		at the present time
*years ago		
		currently
		these days
		in this day and age
		at present
		*nowadays
* = conversational		

EXPLORING THE DOMAIN

At one time, Carmen wanted to be an actress. That was **years ago**. When she was six years old, she told her parents that she was going to be a movie star. She thought movie stars were glamorous.

Now Carmen is 20 years old. **At the present time** she is in college. She is a biology major. Some of her courses are difficult, but they are interesting.

Right now it is exam week. **At this moment** Carmen is taking a final exam in her biology class. She studied hard for it last night. She will probably get a good grade.

Carmen wants to be a scientist. She **recently** changed her major from chemistry to biology. **A short time ago** she visited her parents. They talked about her old wish to be an actress. Carmen laughed. She can't remember wanting to be an actress. In fact, **the other day** she told her best friend that she always wanted to be a scientist.

A long time ago women didn't think about becoming scientists. **At one time** only a few women, such as Madame Curie, worked in the field of science. **These days** things are different. **At present** many young women are studying biology, chemistry, and physics. They are becoming doctors, engineers and research scientists. **Currently**, there are many jobs for women in the sciences.

Exercise 6 *Beginning Practice*

Put the words and phrases in order.

	Past	Recent Past	Present
1. a short time ago at this time some time ago	_____	_____	_____
2. ages ago nowadays the other day	_____	_____	_____

	Past	Recent Past	Present
3. at present			
a short time ago			
a long time ago	_____	_____	_____
4. recently			
at one time			
currently	_____	_____	_____

Exercise 7 *Speaking Practice*

Work with a partner. You cover the domain. Your partner says a word or phrase from the domain. You then tell what is happening or what happened in your country at that time.

Example: **Your partner says:** "at the present time"
                      You say: "At the present time, many people like to listen to rock music."

Exercise 8 *Sense — Nonsense*

Now let's have some fun with these words and phrases. Some of the following sentences are possible. They make sense. Others are not correct or not possible. They don't make sense; they are nonsense.

Circle **Sense** if the sentence makes sense. Circle **Nonsense** if the sentence doesn't make sense. The first one is done for you.

1. At this moment there are not many televisions in the world.

Sense   **Nonsense**

2. The English Department bought a new FAX machine the other day.

Sense   **Nonsense**

3. At this time, electric lights are rare.

Sense   **Nonsense**

4. Some time ago, the only way to cross the ocean was on a ship.

Sense   **Nonsense**

5. Nuclear energy is not currently used to make electricity.

Sense   **Nonsense**

6. Recently, dinosaurs invaded Paris.

Sense   **Nonsense**

Exercise 9 *Word Choice*

Put a phrase from the list below in each blank. More than one phrase may be possible.

a long time ago   the other day   nowadays

these days   right now   years ago

at one time

1. _____ it is easy and inexpensive to make a phone call to another country.

2. _____ dinosaurs lived on the earth.

3. _____ there were no cars. People traveled by horse.

4. _____ Andrew asked his friend to go to a movie.

5. _____ computers are used in many businesses.

6. _____ I am doing a vocabulary exercise.

7. _____ people listened to the radio. There were no televisions.

8. _____ there was a sale at the mall. Jorge bought new shoes.

Exercise 10 *For Writing*

Choose one of the topics below. Write a short paragraph about that topic. Write about change from the past to the present. Use as many words from the domain as you can.

ways of living   smoking   entertainment

roles of women   sports   computers

CHAPTER 3
On Time

GETTING READY Domain 1

1. You have an appointment at the dentist at 1:30 P.M. What time will you arrive? 1:20 P.M.? 1:30 P.M.? 1:40 P.M.?

2. A friend has invited you to dinner at 7:00 P.M. What time will you arrive?

3. How do you feel if you are late for class?

DOMAIN 1

Early or Late?

DR. JOHNSON, DMD
555-1234

YOU HAVE AN APPOINTMENT
ON _April 2_
AT _1:30 P.M._
PLEASE GIVE 24 HOURS NOTICE TO RESCHEDULE

Early	On Time	Late
early	on time	late
	prompt	tardy
	punctual	overdue

EXPLORING THE DOMAIN

Some people in my family like to be on time. They try to be **prompt**. If they have an appointment at 9:00 A.M., they try to arrive at 9:00 or earlier. They know that people who are not **prompt** sometimes have problems.

My brother is always **late**. He never goes to work **early**. When he was in school, he was always **tardy**. His books were often **overdue** at the library. My parents and his teachers tried to teach him to be **on time**, but they didn't succeed. He will never be a **punctual** person.

Exercise 1 *Beginning Practice*

Look at the beginning and ending letters. Then write the correct word in the blank.

1. t_____y = _____

2. p_____l = _____

3. e_____y = _____

4. ov_____e = _____

5. p_____t = _____

6. o____ t_____ = _____

Exercise 2 *Word Choice*

Complete each sentence by writing the best word or phrase in the blank.

1. Jaime is a _____ person. I never have to wait for him.

    tardy   **punctual**   **late**

2. I was _____ yesterday. The teacher was angry. I interrupted the other students when I came in.

    early   **prompt**   **tardy**

3. Trains in Switzerland are usually _____.

    late   **overdue**   **on time**

4. Today is Tuesday. All class projects were due on Monday. Sally is still working on her project. It is _____.

    overdue   **early**   **punctual**

GETTING READY Domain 2

1. Do you know the meanings of these words? Look them up in your dictionary if you need to.

   immediately　　　**soon**　　　**later**　　　**eventually**

2. Imagine that you receive a letter from a friend. When will you answer the letter?

3. Imagine that you cut your finger. When will you put a bandage on it?

DOMAIN 2
The Future

THE FUTURE

Immediately	Soon	Later	Eventually
immediately	soon	later	eventually
at once	shortly	in a while	ultimately
right away	before long	at a later	sometime
this minute	sometime	time	someday
	soon	after a while	one of these days
	in a little while		sooner or later

EXPLORING THE DOMAIN

Exercise 3   *Speaking Practice*

Work with a partner. Your partner says a word or phrase from the domain.
Then you say a word that is similar in meaning. Practice saying as many
words from the domain as you can. Take turns.

Example: **Your partner says:** "before long"
                     You say: "sometime soon"

Exercise 4   *Beginning Practice*

Put each group of words or phrases in the correct order.

	Immediately	Soon	Later	Eventually
1. in a while ultimately shortly this minute	_____	_____	_____	_____
2. sooner or later at once at a later time before long	_____	_____	_____	_____
3. after a while right away sometime sometime soon	_____	_____	_____	_____
4. in a little while immediately someday later	_____	_____	_____	_____

Exercise 5 *Matching*

Hee Kyung is from Korea. She arrived in the U.S. last week. She is a new student at a university. She wrote a list of things she must do. Write a word or phrase from the list on the right in each blank. Discuss your answers with your classmates.

A. 1. find a place to live   _____

   2. graduate from the university   _____

   3. register for classes   _____

   4. join a club   _____

> **at once**
> **sometime soon**
> **at a later time**
> **someday**

B. 1. get a job   _____

   2. write a letter to her parents   _____

   3. buy her textbooks   _____

   4. do her laundry   _____

> **right away**
> **before long**
> **after a while**
> **ultimately**

Exercise 6 *Sense — Nonsense*

Circle **Sense** if the sentence makes sense. Circle **Nonsense** if the sentence doesn't make sense.

1. The phone is ringing. You should answer it sooner or later.

   Sense   **Nonsense**

2. Your mother says that dinner is ready. You should go to the table this minute.

   Sense   **Nonsense**

3. The driver in the car in front of you puts on his brakes. You should slow down eventually.

   Sense   **Nonsense**

4. A piece of food is caught in your friend's throat. He can't breathe. You should call for help immediately.

   Sense   **Nonsense**

5. The bread is baking in the oven. It isn't ready yet. You should check it shortly.

Sense   **Nonsense**

6. There is a fire in the kitchen. You should call the fire department one of these days.

Sense   **Nonsense**

Exercise 7   *For Discussion or Writing*

Choose one of the topics below to write or talk about.

1. You won ten million dollars in the lottery. What will you do immediately? Soon? Later? Eventually? Use as many words from the domain as possible in your answer.

2. You decide to rent a new apartment or buy a new house. What will you do right away? Sometime soon? At a later time? Someday? Use as many words from the domain as possible in your answer.

3. Next month you will have a two-week vacation. You want to plan a trip. What will you do at once? Shortly? After a while? Sometime?

Exercise 8   *For Discussion or Writing*

Do you remember Rebecca Stone? Well, the time management course she took at Peterson Institute was very helpful. Now she owns her own company. Two of her employees are talking. Read the dialogue. Then answer the questions that follow.

Kirsten: Don't forget the meeting tomorrow, Miguel.

Miguel: It will start **around** 9 o'clock, won't it?

Kirsten: I suggest being there at 9 o'clock **sharp**! Rebecca doesn't like employees who are late. She thinks time management is important.

Miguel: Thanks for the suggestion. I'll be there at 9 **on the dot**. By the way, would you like to have lunch together the day after tomorrow?

Kirsten: Sure. Could we meet at the cafeteria **about** noon?

Miguel: That sounds good to me. I'll see you tomorrow at 9!

1. What does Kirsten tell Miguel about their boss, Rebecca Stone?

2. When will Kirsten and Miguel meet for lunch?

3. Imagine that this conversation took place in your country. How would it be different?

2

Let's Eat!

This unit is about *eating*. Eating is important to most people. They like to talk about eating. We talk about times for eating, places for eating, and ways of eating.

CHAPTER 4
What's for Dinner?

GETTING READY Domain 1

1. What do you usually eat in the morning? If you are currently in the U.S., do you eat the same things that you ate in your country?

2. When do you eat your biggest meal of the day?

3. Do you ever eat something between meals? What do you eat?

DOMAIN 1

Meals

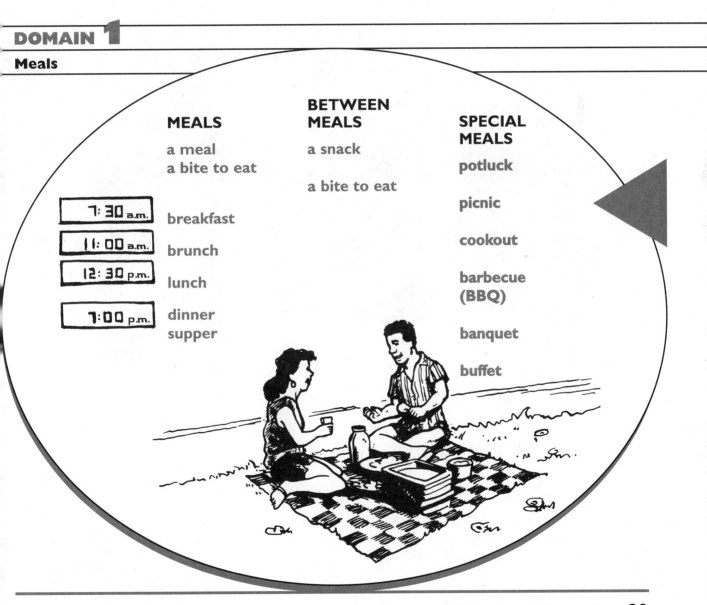

MEALS	BETWEEN MEALS	SPECIAL MEALS
a meal	a snack	potluck
a bite to eat		
	a bite to eat	picnic
7:30 a.m. breakfast		cookout
11:00 a.m. brunch		barbecue (BBQ)
12:30 p.m. lunch		banquet
7:00 p.m. dinner supper		buffet

Walker University Cafeteria

MONDAY - SATURDAY
7:30 - 9:30   **Breakfast**
11:00 - 1:00   **Lunch**
5:30 - 7:00   **Dinner**

SUNDAY
11:00 - 2:00   **Brunch**
6:00 - 7:00   **Supper**

For **a bite to eat** visit the Snack Bar.
You can buy a **snack**
anytime!
Special Events:
Saturday Welcome-back **Picnic**
Sunday **Barbecue**

EXPLORING THE DOMAIN

Students at Walker University eat their **meals** in the university cafeteria. They get three **meals** a day: **breakfast**, **lunch**, and **dinner**.

On Sundays, the students get two **meals**. One is **brunch**. This is a big meal which is **breakfast** and **lunch** together. They can also have **supper**. This is another word for the last **meal** of the day.

Of course, the students get hungry more than three times a day. If they want something to eat between **meals**, they can have a **snack** or **a bite to eat**. They might eat an apple, a cookie, or a piece of candy.

This Saturday, Walker University is having a **picnic**. The cafeteria will serve sandwiches, drinks, and cherry pie outside under some trees. On Sunday, there will be a **barbecue**. At this **cookout**, the students will cook hotdogs and hamburgers on a grill outside.

During the semester, some student clubs have **potlucks**. Everybody brings food to share. **Potlucks** are interesting because people can try different kinds of food.

At the end of the year, there are special events which include a **meal**. There is a **banquet** for honor students. Waiters and waitresses serve the food.

The president of the university has a **buffet** for the professors. The food is put on long tables, and people serve themselves.

Exercise 1 *Beginning Practice*

Work with a partner. Your partner will ask a question, and you will answer it. Take turns.

Example: Your partner says: "When do you have dinner?"
              You say: "I usually have dinner at 6:30."

1. dinner
2. breakfast
3. a snack
4. supper
5. brunch

Exercise 2 *Name the Meal*

A. At what meal do you think an American student eats this food? Write the name of the meal on the line.

1. chicken, rice, broccoli, and apple pie   _____

2. a chocolate chip cookie   _____

3. cereal and orange juice   _____

4. fruit salad, pancakes, bread, eggs, and cheese   _____

5. a hamburger, French fries, and a candy bar   _____

B. Work with a partner. Your partner tells what he or she usually eats at a particular meal. You guess what meal it is. Take turns.

Example: Your partner says: "I eat pizza and an apple."
              You say: "That's lunch."

Exercise 3 *Sentence Completion*

Write the name of the special meal in the blank.

buffet   picnic

              banquet

potluck   barbecue

1. At a _____ the food is put on a long table and peo-
    ple help themselves.

2. On the Fourth of July, we have a _____on a blan-
    ket on the grass.

3. A _____ is a formal meal for many people.

---

4. At a _____ different people bring different foods to share.

5. We cook food outside on a grill at a _____.

Exercise 4 *For Discussion or Writing*

We can combine words from this domain to describe special meals. For example a *BBQ Dinner* is an evening meal. At this meal, people eat food that is cooked outside on a grill. Describe the following special meals.

1. a potluck picnic

2. a buffet banquet

3. a picnic supper

4. a buffet brunch

Exercise 5 *Interviews*

Ask a classmate or an American the following questions. Your teacher may ask you to write down your answers.

1. What do you eat for breakfast?

2. When do you have lunch?

3. Where do you usually eat dinner?

4. What do people in your country usually eat for a snack?

5. Do you cook your own meals?

6. Do you like to go on picnics? Where do you go?

GETTING READY Domain 2

1. Where can a university student go to eat when the cafeteria is closed?

2. Do you like to eat out or at home? Why?

3. What are the names of some restaurants that you like? What kind of food do they serve?

DOMAIN 2

Places to Eat

restaurant
cafeteria
fast-food restaurant

coffee shop
café
bar

snack bar
snack machine
vending machine

hot-dog stand
refreshment stand

EXPLORING THE DOMAIN

When the **cafeteria** at Walker University is closed, some students go out to a **restaurant** or a **coffee shop.** A **coffee shop** is a small **restaurant** that serves light meals. Hotels and motels often have them.

In the spring and summer, students at Walker University enjoy sitting outside at sidewalk **cafés**. These are small restaurants that serve light meals and drinks. Some students like getting a meal to eat at their neighborhood **bar**. They can also get alcoholic beverages if they are 21 or older.

One of the most popular places to eat is a **fast-food restaurant**. At the present time, they are all over the world. The food is prepared quickly, and it is not expensive.

In the city, people often eat lunch "on the run". They want a quick, cheap meal. In some cities, you can find small carts where a street vendor sells hot dogs, pretzels, drinks, and snack food. These **hot-dog stands** are popular with busy office workers.

Tourists eat at **hot-dog stands**, too. People can also buy fast food and snacks at **refreshment stands** and **snack bars** near famous places to visit.

At Walker University and in most offices and public buildings you can find **snack machines** or **vending machines**. People put money in the machine and can buy anything, from a hamburger to chewing gum.

Exercise 6 *Beginning Practice*

Put the letters in the correct order to make a word from this domain. Write the word in the blank.

1. arb _____

2. stunerraat _____

3. sknac chamein _____

4. freetacia _____

5. feecof posh _____

6. tho-odg danst _____

Exercise 7 *Speaking Practice*

What kind of food do people eat at these places? Tell your teacher or another student.

1. a restaurant
2. a cafeteria
3. a hot-dog stand
4. a table next to a snack machine
5. a fast-food restaurant
6. a café

Exercise 8 *Sentence Completion*

Write the best word or phrase from the domain in the blank.

1. I put two quarters in the _____ and bought a candy bar for a snack.

2. The weather is nice today. Let's eat dinner outside at a _____.

3. I really enjoyed seeing the Air and Space Museum. Now I'm really hungry. Maybe we can find a _____ around here.

4. Some students work in the university _____. They help prepare and serve the food.

5. You can't go into that _____. You have to be 21 years old.

6. McDonald's, Wendy's, and Burger King are popular _____. They are in almost every city in the United States!

Exercise 9 *For Discussion or Writing*

Work in a group to answer these questions.

1. What is your favorite restaurant? Why do you like it?
2. Does your school have a cafeteria? Do you like to eat there? Why or why not?
3. What is your favorite fast-food restaurant? Why do you like it?
4. Does your school have vending machines? Where are they? Describe the food that they sell.
5. What is a pizzeria? What are the names of some other places to eat?

CHAPTER 5
Eat, Drink, and Think . . .

GETTING READY Domain 1

1. How do you eat a hamburger?

2. What do you do with gum?

3. How do you eat when you're not very hungry?

DOMAIN 1

The Eating Process

bite
take a bite (of)
bite into

chew

swallow

digest

Exercise 1 *Beginning Practice*

Write the best word or phrase in the blank.

1. First, I _____ my food.

2. Second, I _____ it.

3. Then, I _____ it.

4. After that, my stomach _____ it.

Exercise 2 *Sentence Completion*

Write the best word or phrase in the blank.

> **digest**
> **swallow**
> **chew**
> **take a bite of**

1. Is it hard to _____ gum and talk at the same time?

2. When children _____ something they don't like, they usually make a funny face.

3. Some doctors say that you should _____ your food ten times before you _____ it. This makes it easy for your stomach to _____ it.

4. It's hard to _____ a steak when it is cooked too long.

5. Most fish have bones. When you eat fish you should _____carefully. You don't want to _____ the bones.

Exercise 3 *For Writing or Discussion*

1. What are some foods that people don't chew?

2. What do you do when you take a bite of something that tastes bad? Act it out. What do you say?

3. What is one food that is difficult for people to digest?

GETTING READY Domain 2

1. When do you eat quickly? When do you eat slowly?

2. When do you eat a lot? When do you eat a little?

3. How do you eat an ice cream cone? How do you drink hot tea or coffee?

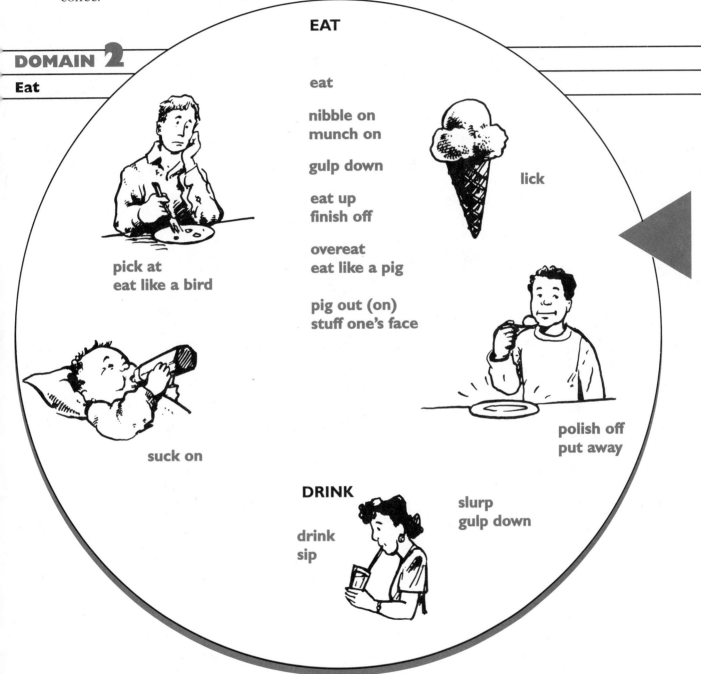

EAT

eat

nibble on
munch on

gulp down

eat up
finish off

overeat
eat like a pig

pig out (on)
stuff one's face

lick

pick at
eat like a bird

polish off
put away

suck on

DRINK

drink
sip

slurp
gulp down

EXPLORING THE DOMAIN

It's final exam week at Fullerton College. Many students are nervous. Some students eat a lot when they feel nervous. That is Mike's problem. He always **overeats** when he has a big test. In fact, he **eats like a pig**. Of course, no one says that to his face because it would be rude!

Last night, he ate a steak, a baked potato, and five slices of bread. Then he **pigged out on** three pieces of banana cream pie with vanilla ice cream. That wasn't enough! He **stuffed his face** with half a box of chocolates.

The day before yesterday he **ate up** a whole box of chocolates while he was studying for his biology exam. After he **finished off** that box, he **polished off** a half-gallon of ice cream. He **put away** enough food for a week in just one night.

His friend, Mark, has the opposite problem. When he is nervous he hardly eats at all. The day before his chemistry exam he **ate like a bird**. He **picked at** his food with his fork, but he didn't really eat very much. He **nibbled on** a carrot. That was all he **munched on** all day.

Mark and Mike are really different. Mike likes to put his spoon in the peanut butter jar and **lick** the spoon. Mark hates peanut butter. He prefers cottage cheese.

When Mark is thirsty he likes to **drink** milk. He drinks a little at a time. He **sips** his milk slowly. Then for dessert, all he has is a piece of hard candy. He puts it in his mouth and **sucks on** it.

Mike likes milk too. He likes it in big strawberry milkshakes. He drinks them noisily. He **slurps**. He also drinks them very quickly. Yesteray afternoon, he **gulped down** a milkshake in one minute!

Mark and Mike will both be glad when final exam week is over. Then they can relax. Maybe Mark will stop **picking at** his food, and Mike will stop **overeating**.

Exercise 4 *Beginning Practice*

Put the words in the correct column.

Eat	Drink
1. _____	1. _____
2. _____	2. _____
3. _____	3. _____
4. _____	
5. _____	

> **nibble on**
> **slurp**
> **pick at**
> **munch on**
> **gulp down**
> **sip**
> **pig out**

Exercise 5 *More Beginning Practice*

Write the correct phrase in the blank.

1. a lot   _____

2. a little   _____

3. quickly   _____

4. all of it   _____

5. with noise   _____

> **eat like a bird**
> **polish off**
> **slurp**
> **gulp down**
> **stuff one's face**

GRAMMAR GUIDE

Read the following sentences outloud. Notice how they are different.

I gulp down my breakfast.
I gulp my breakfast down.
I gulp it down.

I will polish off the pizza.
I will polish the pizza off.
I will polish it off.

She always munches on chips before dinner.
She always munches on them before dinner.

Exercise 6 *Sentence Completion*

Choose the best phrase and write it in the blank.

A. 1. People who eat like pigs eat a lot. They often eat quickly too.

Some people _____. They

_____ without even thinking

about it.

    a. pig out on them   **b.** pig out on a whole bag of potato chips

2. A mouse likes to _____. He

_____ in the kitchen while every-

body is sleeping.

    a. nibble on cheese   **b.** nibbles on it

3. Miguel had a terrible cold and a cough. The doctor told him to

_____. After he

_____, his throat felt better.

    a. suck on a cough drop   **b.** sucked on it

4. Tina doesn't like to try new things. Whenever her husband cooks

a new dish for her, she _____.

Last night, he made a new kind of spaghetti. She

_____ and left most of it on her

plate.

    a. picked at the spaghetti   **b.** picks at it

5. At a movie, people like to _____.

They _____ before, during, and

sometimes after the movie!

    a. munch on snacks   **b.** munch on them

B. **1.** Eric likes to _____

_____ every week. He _____

_____ in less than 15 minutes. His roommate is shocked. He said,

"What???!! You _____ in less

than 15 minutes? I can't believe it!"

  a. polishes off a carton of ice cream

  b. polish it off

  c. polish a carton of ice cream off

2. On Thanksgiving, Americans _____

_____. They _____

_____, but there is always some left. Some cooks say, "Please!

_____ because I don't

want to have any leftovers!"

  a. eat up lots of turkey and pumpkin pie

  b. Eat the turkey up

  c. eat it up

3. We only have a few minutes for lunch. Let's go to the fastfood

restaurant and _____. It

isn't good to _____. But, if

we _____ fast enough, we

can go shopping later.

  a. gulp them down

  b. gulp a hamburger and some fries down

  c. gulp down a hamburger and some fries

4. Nui: "I'm so happy. You gave me a box of chocolates for Valentine's Day. They were delicious!

I _____ last night."

Wichit: "Well, the next time I give you a box of chocolates, I want to eat some before you _____ !"

Nui: "Okay. Next Valentine's Day, I'll give you some before I

_____."

   a. finished the box of chocolates off

   b. finish them off

   c. finish off the box of chocolates

5. Teenagers need a lot of energy. They _____

_____. At one meal, some teenagers _____

_____. After they _____

_____, they want more!

   a. put away enough food for a small army

   b. put it away

   c. put a lot of food away

Exercise 7 *Speaking Practice*

Work with a partner. Use a word from the domain to tell how you eat these foods. Take turns.

Example: Your partner says: "How do you drink a vanilla milkshake?"
               You say: "I slurp it down."

1. How do you eat a chocolate ice cream cone?

2. How do you eat a hamburger?

3. How do you eat something that you really enjoy?

4. How do you eat something that you don't like?

5. How do you eat a bag of potato chips?

6. How do you eat when you are very hungry?

7. How do you eat when you are not very hungry?

Exercise 8 *Rhyming Words*

Fill in the blank with a word from the domain that rhymes with the word
in italics.

1. I like to stop and _____

   My ice cream on a *stick*.

2. What do you want to *lunch on?*

   What would you like to _____?

3. If food is rich and *sweet*

   I want to _____.

4. When eating soup, he always _____.

   And when he's done, he always *burps!*

5. I have an old friend, I give you my *word*.

   She's big as a house, but she _____ _____

   _____ _____.

   And she has a daughter who's not very *big*.

   She's a tiny young girl, but she _____ _____

   _____ _____.

6. My son always asks, "What's for lunch *today?*"

   Whatever you give him, he'll _____ it _____.

7. Pepper on my food makes me *cough*.

   That's why I never _____ it _____.

Exercise 9 Sense or Nonsense?

Circle **Sense** if the sentence makes sense. Circle **Nonsense** if the sentence doesn't make sense.

1. He makes a lot of noise when he drinks his coffee. He slurps it from his cup.

   Sense   **Nonsense**

2. This cheesecake is delicious. Can I have more? I've already polished off the first piece.

   Sense   **Nonsense**

3. Aren't you hungry? You never eat anything at all. Why do you always eat like a pig?

   Sense   **Nonsense**

4. Doctors say that you shouldn't eat very much on an airplane flight. You should eat like a bird.

   Sense   **Nonsense**

5. He always pigs out on pizza. He hates it.

   Sense   **Nonsense**

6. The students only had 20 minutes for lunch. That wasn't enough time. They had to gulp down their food quickly.

   Sense   **Nonsense**

7. There was a pie-eating contest at the fair. One of the older children put away a whole pie in two minutes. She was the winner.

   Sense   **Nonsense**

8. Right now, she's having fried chicken for lunch. She is taking big bites and eating quickly. She is nibbling on the chicken.

   Sense   **Nonsense**

9. I want to lose weight. I'm going to go out and stuff my face with a large pizza and an order of French fries.

   Sense   **Nonsense**

10. Mark always eats a lot during finals week at Fullerton College. He picks at his food.

    Sense   **Nonsense**

Exercise 10 *For Discussion or Writing*

Discuss these questions in a group. Your teacher may ask you to write your answers.

1. Do you know anyone who eats like a bird? What does he or she eat for breakfast?

2. Do you like to nibble on food while you are watching TV? What kind of food do you like to munch on?

3. When you were a child, did you have to eat up everything on your plate? What did your parents do when you didn't finish off your dinner?

4. What's your favorite food? Do you ever pig out on it?

5. On a hot day, when you are very thirsty, what is your favorite drink? How do you drink it? Do you sip it or gulp it down?

6. The title of this chapter is "Eat, Drink, and Think". It is more usual to say, "Eat, Drink, and Be Merry". This is an old saying that means that people should eat delicious food, drink good beverages, and be happy. What do you think about this idea?

7. What is a saying about food, eating, or drinking from your country?

CHAPTER 6
What's Cooking?

GETTING READY Domain 1

1. Everybody eats, but not everybody cooks. Do you cook? What do you cook?

2. Do you know other words in English that mean *cook?*

3. What are some ways that people in your country cook meat?

People around the world eat many different kinds of food. People eat cooked food and uncooked food. They can cook with heat alone, with hot water, with hot oil, or with a microwave.

DOMAIN 1

Cook

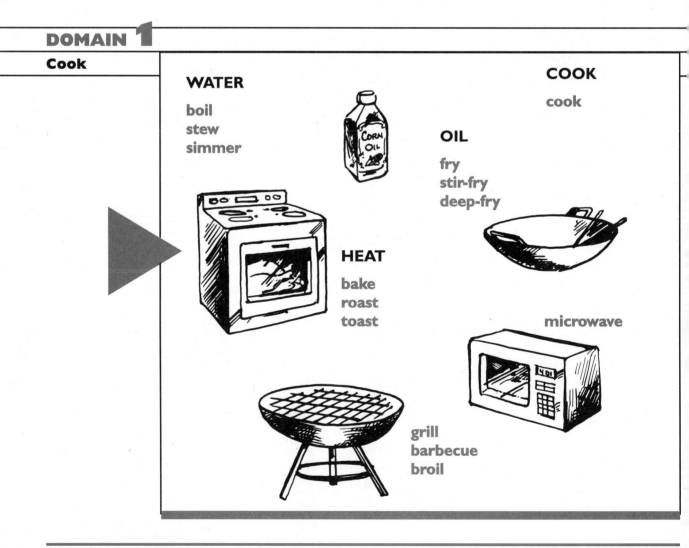

WATER
boil
stew
simmer

COOK
cook

OIL
fry
stir-fry
deep-fry

HEAT
bake
roast
toast

microwave

grill
barbecue
broil

EXPLORING THE DOMAIN

When you **bake** bread, you need an oven. The bread **bakes** in the oven by getting heat from all sides. You can also use an oven to **roast** meat, like chicken or beef.

Many Americans like to cook on a grill. When they **grill**, **broil**, or **barbecue** something, the heat comes from one side. They cook the hamburger on one side, and then they turn it over.

Some people like to **toast** their bread for breakfast. They use a toaster, and the bread turns a light brown on both sides at the same time.

Some people say they don't know how to cook. They only know how to **boil** water. This isn't hard to do! You heat the water until it reaches 212° Fahrenheit. When water **boils**, it creates steam. We use steam to cook vegetables. You can **steam** carrots for three or four minutes.

Soup has to cook for a longer time. We turn the heat down, below the boiling point, and let the soup **simmer** or **stew** for a while.

Many people cook with oil. Some cooks **fry** potatoes and chicken and other kinds of foods. Other cooks like to mix small pieces of meat and vegetables together and **stir-fry** them like the Chinese do. Some other cooks use a lot of oil to cook something in a deep pan. They **deep-fry** foods like French fries and donuts.

These days, more and more people **microwave** their food. It is a fast way to cook some food. It is possible to heat and reheat food in a few minutes.

Exercise 1 *Beginning Practice*

Study the words in the domain. Then circle the best description for each word. Try not to look at the domain. When you are done, check your answers.

1. boil: **with water**   **with oil**   **only with heat**

2. fry: **with water**   **with oil**   **only with heat**

3. grill: **with water**   **with oil**   **only with heat**

4. simmer: **with water**   **with oil**   **only with heat**

5.	deep-fry:	**with water**	**with oil**	**only with heat**
6.	toast:	**with water**	**with oil**	**only with heat**
7.	steam:	**with water**	**with oil**	**only with heat**
8.	stew:	**with water**	**with oil**	**only with heat**
9.	broil:	**with water**	**with oil**	**only with heat**
10.	roast:	**with water**	**with oil**	**only with heat**

Exercise 2 *Word Scramble*

Put the letters in the correct order to make a word from the *Cook* domain.
Write the word in the blank.

1. keab   _____

2. atems   _____

3. creabeub   _____

4. tris-fyr   _____

5. wraceovim   _____

6. obil   _____

7. reimsm   _____

8. otats   _____

Exercise 3 *Sentence Completion*

Complete the sentence with the best word.

1. When you make tea, you should _____ the water.

   toast   **boil**

2. This bean soup needs to cook for several hours. You should
   _____ it on the stove.

   simmer   **fry**

3. It's too hot to cook a big meal. Let's just _____ this
   frozen dinner.

   steam   **microwave**

---

4. When you _____ these onions, please don't use too much oil.

stew   **fry**

5. I think this fish will be delicious if we _____ it outside on the barbecue.

grill   **bake**

6. Thanksgiving is an important American holiday. On Thanksgiving Day, I always _____ a big turkey for my family.

broil   **roast**

7. My mother likes to cook Chinese food. She likes to _____beef and snowpeas.

stir-fry   **stew**

8. This kind of meat is very tough. To make it soft and tender, you need to _____ it for several hours.

stew   **broil**

9. I don't want to eat cold bread. Let's _____ two slices and make a sandwich.

steam   **toast**

Exercise 4 *Interviews*

Ask an American or a group of your classmates the following questions.

1. What are some foods you can bake?
2. What foods can you boil?
3. What foods can you fry?
4. What foods can you steam?

GRAMMAR GUIDE

We use the words for *Cook* to make adjectives that describe food. The adjectives tell us how the food was cooked. For example, we say:

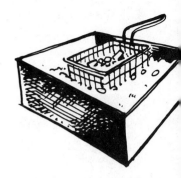

fried chicken
baked fish
boiled potatoes

We form these adjectives with the past participle of the verb.

However, the word *roast* is different. We say:

roast turkey
roast beef
roasted peanuts

Exercise 5 *Sentence Completion*

Write the correct adjective.

A. **Example:** The cafeteria at Washington University serves ___baked___ *(bake)* potatoes for lunch and dinner.

1. At a famous restaurant in New York, they serve wonderful _____ *(grill)* chicken.

2. This morning I had breakfast at a coffee shop near my house. I had a _____*(toast)* bagel with cream cheese.

3. These _____ *(steam)* vegetables aren't very good. They are soft and they have no taste.

4. The flight attendants gave everybody little bags of _____ *(roast)* peanuts.

5. Do you like to put _____ *(stew)* tomatoes in your spaghetti sauce?

6. My mother makes delicious _____ *(barbecue)* chicken. It has a spicy tomato sauce on it.

7. We stayed in the mountains for one week. We had to boil the water because it wasn't safe to drink. We drank the _____ *(boil)* water after it got cold.

B. Choose a word from the domain and write the correct adjective.

1. We ordered _____ mixed vegetables and _____ rice at the Chinese restaurant.

2. For breakfast, I want two _____ eggs and a _____ English muffin.

3. For lunch, I want a _____ cheese sandwich and a salad.

4. For dinner, I will eat some _____ chicken and a _____ potato.

5. Americans often eat _____ potatoes. They are called French fries.

GETTING READY Domain 2

1. Do you like your vegetables cooked or uncooked?

2. What happens if food is cooked too long?

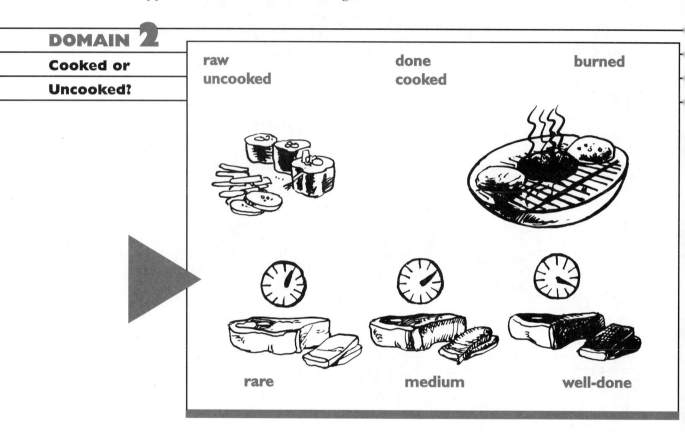

raw
uncooked

done
cooked

burned

rare

medium

well-done

EXPLORING THE DOMAIN

We cook some foods for a long time and some foods for a short time. We don't cook other foods at all. We eat them **uncooked** or **raw**. For example, many people like **raw** vegetables, like carrots or cucumbers. What other foods do people eat **raw**?

Most people cook meat. They think **uncooked** meat is dangerous. It can make people sick.

Some people think beef is done when it is still very pink on the inside. They like **rare** hamburgers. Other people like **medium** hamburgers. They are a little pink on the inside, but brown on the outside. Other people want hamburgers that are brown on the inside and the outside. They like **well-done** hamburgers. How do you like your hamburgers?

If a hamburger is left on the grill too long, it burns. A **burned** hamburger is black and tastes terrible. Nobody wants to eat it.

Exercise 6 *Beginning Practice*

Put the words in the correct order from *Uncooked* to *Cooked*. Write the words in the blanks.

UNCOOKED ══════════════▶ COOKED

1. medium raw burned _____ _____ _____

2. well-done uncooked rare _____ _____ _____

3. burned uncooked medium _____ _____ _____

Exercise 7 *Sentence Completion*

Write a word from the domain that is similar to the word(s) in parentheses.

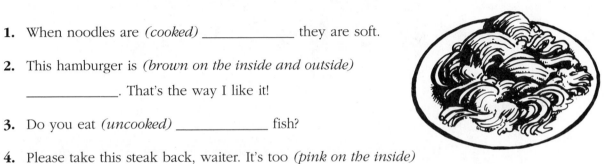

1. When noodles are *(cooked)* _____ they are soft.

2. This hamburger is *(brown on the inside and outside)* _____. That's the way I like it!

3. Do you eat *(uncooked)* _____ fish?

4. Please take this steak back, waiter. It's too *(pink on the inside)* _____ for me!

Exercise 8 *Sense or Nonsense?*

Circle **Sense** if the sentence makes sense. Circle **Nonsense** if the sentence doesn't make sense.

1. Many people like to eat raw carrots.	**Sense**	**Nonsense**
2. I think the bread is done. It's light brown on the top.	**Sense**	**Nonsense**
3. This hamburger is burned. Everybody will like it.	**Sense**	**Nonsense**
4. This steak is well-done. It's still pink on the inside.	**Sense**	**Nonsense**
5. The Japanese like to eat raw fish. They call it *sashimi*.	**Sense**	**Nonsense**
6. Don't eat uncooked eggs in the U.S. You might get sick.	**Sense**	**Nonsense**

3

It's a Material World

This unit is about *things*. Many people care about the things around them. They talk about what they are made of, how they break, and how to fix them.

Chapter 7
What Is This Stuff?

GETTING READY Domain 1

1. What is the earth made of?

2. What are some natural things in our world?

3. What are some manmade things in our world?

matter
material
substance

EXPLORING THE DOMAIN

Matter is anything that takes up space: solid, liquid, or gas. All of the **material** on the earth is natural or manmade. Water and wool are examples of natural **substances**. Paper and plastic are examples of manmade products. Technology helps us make new and better **substances** like cement, steel, and plastic. These **substances** are important to us. They make our lives easier, but we need to be careful. Some of these manmade **materials** are bad for the earth.

Exercise 1 *Beginning Practice*

Look at the beginning and ending letters. Write the correct word from the domain.

1. m_____l   =   _____

2. m_____r   =   _____

3. s_____e   =   _____

Exercise 2 *Sentence Completion*

Write the best word from the domain.

1. Cement is a very hard s_____. It is used to make side-walks and buildings.

2. For scientists, m_____r is anything that takes up space. It can be solid, liquid, or gas.

3. Honey is a sweet, sticky s_____.

4. Steel is a strong, manmade m_____l. Car makers use it to make cars.

5. Albert Einstein showed that m_____r can be changed into energy. ($E = mc^2$)

6. After the earthquake, people wanted to rebuild their houses and businesses. Building m_____ls were in high demand.

GETTING READY Domain 2

1. How did people live 5,000 years ago? How did they cook? How did they make their houses?

2. What kind of matter is there in a desert?

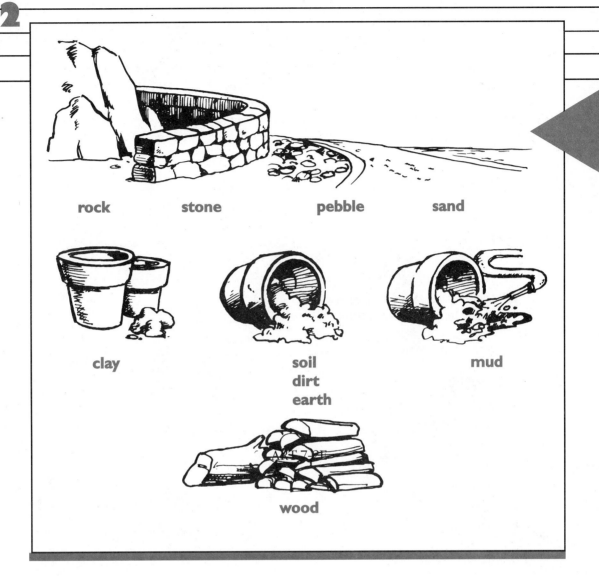

rock   stone   pebble   sand

clay

soil
dirt
earth

mud

wood

EXPLORING THE DOMAIN

Thousands of years ago, people used natural materials to make tools, build houses, and prepare food. They made tools out of bones, **rocks**, **stones**, and **wood**. They used the **stone** tools to make arrows. They used these arrows to hunt and kill animals.

Early humans burned **wood** to keep warm and to cook. They roasted meat or fish on flat **stones**. Sometimes they used hot **stones** to boil water. Later, people used **clay** to make pots for cooking.

Prehistoric people used **stone** tools to cut down trees. They used **wood** from trees to make simple houses. Other early humans built houses from

grass, **stones**, or **mud** baked hard by the sun. Some of them mixed the **mud** with small **stones** or **pebbles**. Most of their houses had hard **dirt** floors. These **dirt** floors sometimes turned to **mud** when it rained.

People eventually learned to plant crops and to work the **earth**. They began to use animals to help them with their work. They built their houses in places where the **soil** was good. Good **soil** is rich and not too hard. It contains more than just **dirt** or **earth**. It also has **sand** (very small pieces of rock), **clay**, dead leaves, and twigs (very small pieces of **wood**).

Exercise 3 *Beginning Practice*

Write a word from the domain that has a similar meaning.

Example: rock   *stone*
_____

1. small, smooth rock   _____

2. rock that is broken into very,
   very small pieces (grains)   _____

3. dirt for growing plants   _____

4. wet dirt   _____

5. material that dries very hard
   when heated   _____

6. material that comes from trees   _____

7. dirt   _____

8. material used for making pots   _____

9. material that burns   _____

Exercise 4 *For Discussion or Writing*

Answer each question using words from the domain.

1. What materials can you find in a garden?

2. What substances can you find at the beach?

3. What substances can you use to make a wall or a fence?

Exercise 5 *Sentence Completion*

Write the best word from the domain in the blank.

1. There's a hole in the ground. Let's fill it up with _____.

2. People have used this material to make walls for centuries. A wall that is made of _____ is very strong.

3. In the Amazon rain forest, the _____ is very thin. When people cut down trees, it washes away.

4. After a heavy rain, there is a lot of _____ everywhere. You should wear boots when you go outside.

5. Long ago, people used an hourglass to tell time. It had two parts. One part was filled with _____. When a person turned it over, the _____ went slowly into the other part.

6. _____ climbing is a sport that people like to do in the mountains. You need special equipment and strong arms and legs.

7. Some people like plastic flower pots better than _____ones. They say that the _____ ones take water away from the plants. The plants become too dry.

8. The northwestern part of the United States has a lot of pine trees. The _____ from the pine trees is used as a building material all over the U.S.

Exercise 6 *Sense or Nonsense*

Circle **Sense** if the sentences makes sense. Circle **Nonsense** if it does not.

1. This soil is very good. It has lots of rocks in it.

    Sense   **Nonsense**

2. Thousands of years ago, people made houses of dried mud.

    Sense   **Nonsense**

3. Some people take their shoes off inside their houses. They don't want to get dirt on their floors.

    Sense   **Nonsense**

4. This earth has too much sand in it. We can't grow very much here.

    Sense   **Nonsense**

5. In cold climates, people make houses out of wood. These wooden houses have stone roofs.

    Sense   **Nonsense**

6. If you heat wood, it becomes hard.

    Sense   **Nonsense**

Exercise 7 *For Discussion or Writing*

Look at the following sentences. What do the underlined words mean?

1. I like to use sandy soil for my desert plants. They grow well in it.

2. This is such a rocky cliff that I'm afraid to climb it.

3. Don't drink that muddy water! It might make you sick!

4. Look at this dirty floor. I should clean it before my mother comes over.

GETTING READY Domain 3

1. What are you wearing right now? What is it made of? Do you read the label in a piece of clothing before you buy it?

2. What did people wear 5,000 years ago?

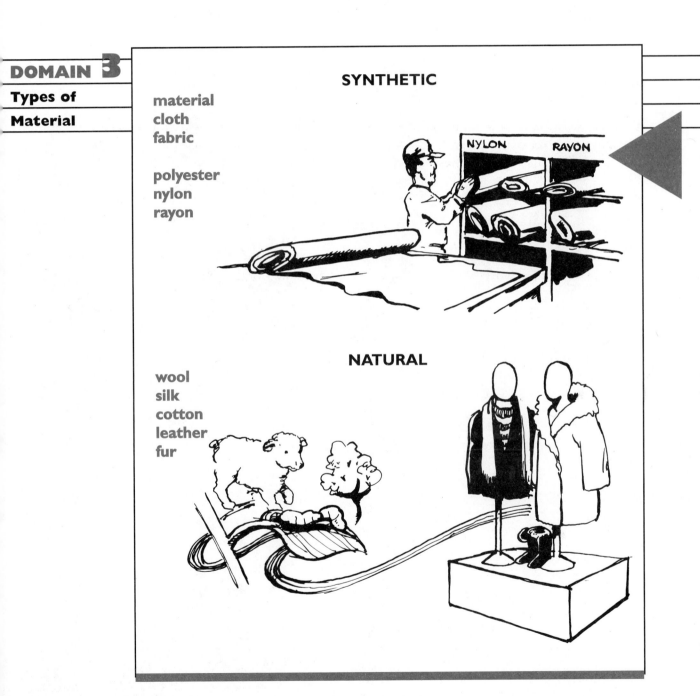

DOMAIN 3

Types of Material

material
cloth
fabric

polyester
nylon
rayon

wool
silk
cotton
leather
fur

SYNTHETIC

NYLON   RAYON

NATURAL

EXPLORING THE DOMAIN

In 1991, some German tourists found something very surprising in the Alps, near the border between Austria and Italy. They saw something in the ice. They didn't know what it was.

Now, researchers know what they found. They found the body of a man who was 5,000 years old. The ice had protected his body, his clothes, and the stuff he was carrying.

The iceman's clothes were made of animal skins. He had a grass cape, and his shoes were made of **leather**.

Today we use some of the same materials that the iceman did. We wear **leather** shoes and **leather** coats. Some people wear coats made of **fur**.

We don't wear grass capes anymore. These days, large textile factories use machines to make many different kinds of **cloth**. Today, we have clothes that are made of natural **fabrics** like **cotton** (from a plant), **wool** (from sheep), and **silk** (from an insect). Synthetic **materials** like **polyester**, **rayon**, and **nylon** are usually not as expensive as natural **fabrics**.

Exercise 8 *Beginning Practice*

Put the letters in the correct order to make a word from the domain. Write the word.

Example: owlo _____ wool _____

1. thaleer _____

2. ruf _____

3. thloc _____

4. lonny _____

5. tramalie _____

6. liks _____

7. stoelyper _____

8. crafib _____

9. toontc _____

10. onary _____

Exercise 9 *Matching*

Write the fabric next to the substance that is used to make it.

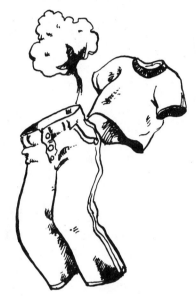

cotton
wool
rayon
silk
nylon
polyester

1. the fur of sheep   _____

2. synthetic chemicals   _____

                                        _____

                                        _____

3. small threads made by an insect   _____

4. soft, white substance that grows
   around the seed of a plant   _____

Exercise 10 *For Discussion or Writing*

Answer these questions.

1. What clothes are made of cotton?

2. What clothes are made of wool?

3. What is made of nylon?

4. What fabrics are good for summer? What fabrics are good for winter?

5. What materials are expensive? Which ones are cheap?

6. What are some other kinds of material that are used to make clothes?

GETTING READY Domain 4

1. What was the Iron Age?

2. What are grocery bags made of?

DOMAIN 4
Other Materials

concrete
cement

brick

metal

glass

plastic

paper
cardboard

rubber

iron (Fe)
copper (Cu)
aluminum (Al)
steel

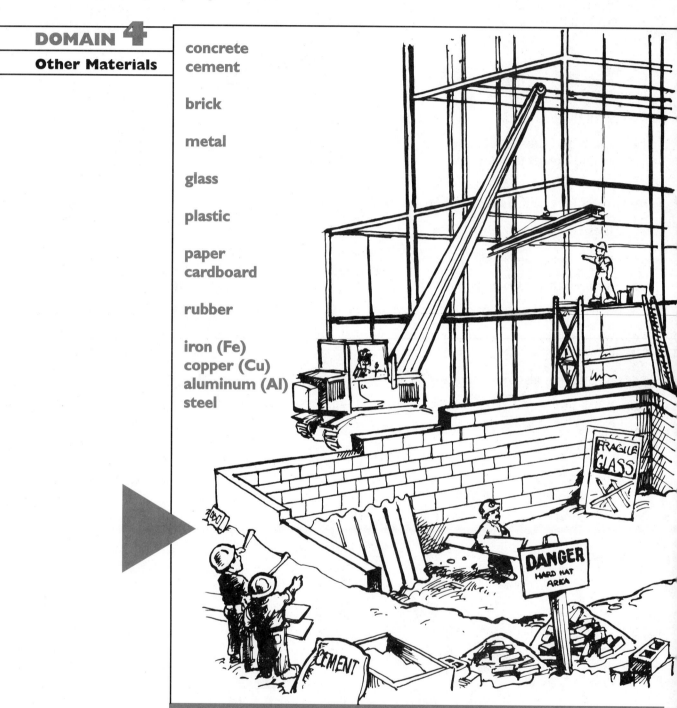

EXPLORING THE DOMAIN

The iceman is very old. He tells us about life in the Iron Age. Near his body, scientists found four long sticks made of wood. Maybe he wanted to use them to make spears or a shelter.

The iceman had an ax in his hand. It was made of copper, a strong and unusual **metal** for that time. He also had a needle made of bone and some tools for sharpening hard rocks and stones.

How much has human life changed in 5,000 years? We have many of the same natural resources and materials that the iceman had. The biggest change is that we have more manmade products.

These days, we still make houses out of wood, but we also use manmade building materials, such as **concrete**, **cement**, and **bricks**.

Like the iceman, we have metal tools. But today, we have many more kinds of **metal** and use them in many more ways. Soft drink companies make cans out of **aluminum.** Car companies make automobile bodies out of **steel**. Humans learned to make **glass**. We use **glass** for windows, doors, and dishes.

Glass breaks very easily, so now we also have **plastic**. Many of the things we buy and use have **plastic** in them. Look around the room. What are some things that are made with **plastic? Plastic** can be very strong and hard, or it can be soft and easy-to-bend (flexible). There are many different kinds of **plastic**. Styrofoam and vinyl are two examples.

We have **paper** and lots of it. We use it for making books and wrapping packages. We use **paper** to make **cardboard**, a heavy brown **paper** product. Many of the things that we buy at the grocery store are in **cardboard** boxes. Americans throw away tons of **paper** every year. They also throw away a lot of **cardboard**.

Garbage dumps are full of **paper**, **glass**, and **metal**. This is bad for the earth. Many people around the world are trying to do something about this problem.

Exercise 11 *Beginning Practice*

Write words from the domain that are used to make these things.

Example: a book: ____*paper*____ and ____*cardboard*____

1. the walls of a house: b_____, c_____, and

   c_____

2. an alarm clock: m_____, p_____, and
g_____

3. a bicycle wheel: r_____ and m_____

4. a doll for children: p_____

5. a photo album: p_____, p_____, and
c_____

Exercise 12 Sentence Completion

Write the name of the substance that each thing is made of. A word may be used more than once.

| cardboard |
| concrete |
| plastic |
| glass |
| brick |
| cement |
| metal |
| rubber |
| paper |

1. A sidewalk is made of _____.

2. A bottle is made of _____ or _____.

3. Many erasers are made of _____.

4. A paper clip is made of _____ or _____.

5. A cereal box is made of _____.

6. A Japanese origami bird is made of folded _____.

7. Children's toys are often made of brightly-colored _____.

8. One hundred years ago, many buildings in American cities were made of _____ and _____.

Exercise 13 *For Writing or Discussion*

Answer these questions.

1. What are some other metals that you know? What are some things that people make out of these metals?

2. What are some fabrics that you know?

3. What are some kinds of plastic that you know?

4. What are two important things that people make out of glass?

5. Why is rubber a good material for car tires?

6. Do you think that we will use more **paper** in the future or less? Why?

Exercise 14 *Matching*

Write the word from the domain that tells what these materials make.

1. melted sand   _____

2. gravel (tiny stones), sand and cement   _____

3. baked clay   _____

4. chemicals from oil and coal   _____

5. wood or cloth   _____

> glass
> concrete
> **brick**
> **plastic**
> **paper**

Exercise 15 *Discussion: Natural or Manmade?*

Look at these words from the domain. Discuss whether the material is manmade or natural.

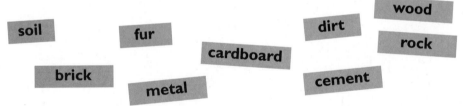

soil   fur   wood   dirt   rock   cardboard   brick   metal   cement

Exercise 16 *For Reading, then Discussion or Writing*

Recycling
Technology gives us many manmade **substances**. These manmade **substances** help us and make our lives easier. However, they can also hurt the earth. Nowadays, people use and throw away too much **paper**, **metal**, **glass**, and **plastic**. In addition, the burning of **plastic** makes the air dirty. Making new **paper** uses too many trees. Making **metal** cans uses a lot of energy.

People are trying to find ways to use these **materials** again. Right now, many cities have places where you can take your old **paper**, **metal**, **glass**, and **plastic**. These places recycle your trash. They make new **materials** out of the old **materials**.

Can these things be recycled? Do people in your country recycle these things? Work in a small group to answer these questions. Put a check mark in the correct column of each list.

	People Can Recycle		People Do Recycle	
	YES	NO	YES	NO
a. aluminum soda cans	☐	☐	☐	☐
b. cardboard boxes	☐	☐	☐	☐
c. office paper	☐	☐	☐	☐
d. glass bottles	☐	☐	☐	☐
e. plastic beverage bottles	☐	☐	☐	☐
f. plastic grocery bags	☐	☐	☐	☐
g. car batteries	☐	☐	☐	☐
h. light bulbs	☐	☐	☐	☐
i. toothpaste tubes	☐	☐	☐	☐
j. newspapers	☐	☐	☐	☐
k. magazines	☐	☐	☐	☐
l. food	☐	☐	☐	☐
m. eyeglasses	☐	☐	☐	☐
n. wooden furniture	☐	☐	☐	☐
o. aerosol cans	☐	☐	☐	☐
p. telephone books	☐	☐	☐	☐

Exercise 17 *For Writing or Discussion*

The title of this chapter is, "What Is This Stuff?". *Stuff* is a word that we use a lot. It can mean any substance. For example, people say, "I don't have the stuff we need for the picnic." Here, *"stuff"* might mean: barbecued chicken, paper napkins, or plastic forks and spoons.

We can use it about the characteristics of people, too. The title of both a book and a movie about some of the first American astronauts is called, "The Right Stuff". We can say, "He has the right stuff to be an astronaut." This means that someone has the right characteristics and abilities to be an astronaut.

Look at the following sentences. What does the word stuff mean in each sentence?

1. Why don't you bring that stuff over, and we'll build a bookshelf in the living room.

2. I don't have enough of this stuff to make a long skirt. Maybe I can make a shirt.

3. He doesn't have the right stuff to be a lawyer. For one thing, he's not very smart.

4. What kind of stuff do you like to eat for breakfast?

Chapter 8
Putting It All Together

GETTING READY Domain 1

1. Do you like to put things together (like a model airplane or a ship in a bottle)?

2. Do you know anyone who likes to put things together? Describe the steps for putting something together.

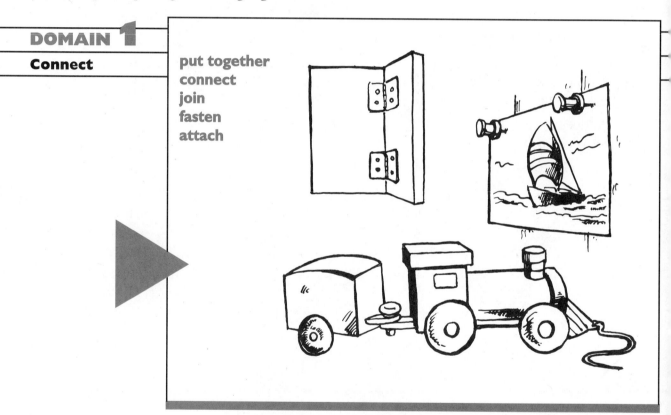

put together
connect
join
fasten
attach

EXPLORING THE DOMAIN

This chapter is about **putting** things **together**. You can make a lot of different things when you **join** two pieces of wood or **fasten** wheels to a piece of steel. How do you **attach** a poster to a wall? Have you ever **connected** shapes to make a picture?

That's what you are going to do in this activity. This is a tangram, a game that comes from China. There are seven geometric shapes: five triangles, a rhomboid, and a square. You **connect** these shapes in different ways to make many different pictures.

Cut out the shapes below. (You may want to photocopy them first.) Then, work with a partner to see if you can **join** the pieces to make the house and the two people in the boat. It is not as easy to **put** the pieces **together** as it looks! The answers are on page 88.

When you finish, save your tangram. **Fasten** it to a piece of cardboard. Use tape or glue. Then **attach** the tangram to the wall of your classroom. You can also put the pieces together in other ways to make new pictures. Your classmates can try to solve your tangrams.

Exercise 1 *Beginning Practice*

Write the words from the domain.

1. p_____ t_____ = _____

2. j_____ = _____

3. f_____ = _____

4. a_____ = _____

Exercise 2 *Sentence Completion*

Write a word from the domain in the blank.

1. There are lots of ways to p_____ two pieces of paper
   t_____. For example, you can use a paper clip or a
   stapler.

2. On an airplane, the passengers have to f_____ their
   seatbelts before the plane takes off.

3. Do you know how to c_____ a computer to a printer?

4. We're going on a long trip this summer. We have to carry a lot of
   things with us. We should a_____ a trailer to our car.

5. How can you j_____ two pieces of rope together? It's
   easy, just tie a knot!

GETTING READY Domain 2

1. What do people use to put things together? Bring in as many items as you can find. Discuss them in class.

2. How are the items alike? How are they different? Put them in similar groups.

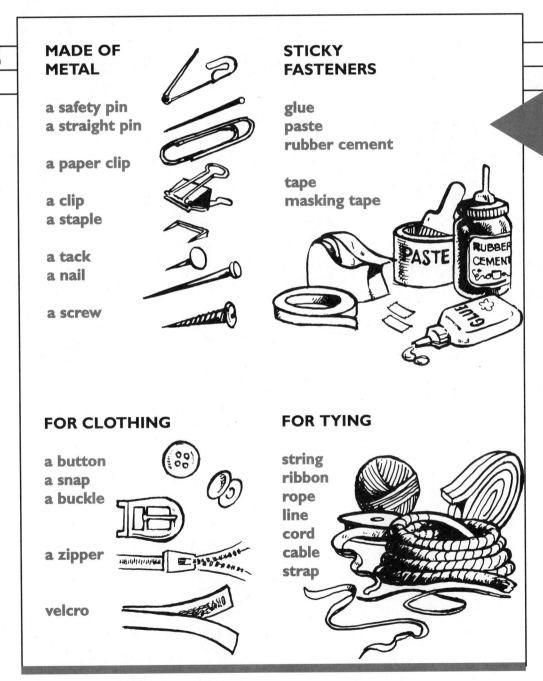

MADE OF METAL

a safety pin
a straight pin

a paper clip

a clip
a staple

a tack
a nail

a screw

STICKY FASTENERS

glue
paste
rubber cement

tape
masking tape

FOR CLOTHING

a button
a snap
a buckle

a zipper

velcro

FOR TYING

string
ribbon
rope
line
cord
cable
strap

Made of Metal

Exercise 3 *Beginning Practice*

Look at each drawing and write the name of the object.

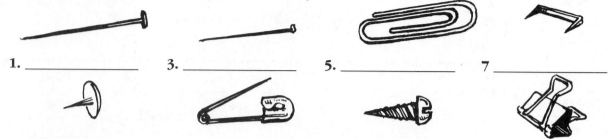

1. _____   3. _____   5. _____   7 _____

2. _____   4. _____   6. _____   8 _____

Exercise 4 *More Beginning Practice*

Write the best word in the blank.

nail   tack   paper clip   screw   safety pin   staple   straight pin

1. Use a _____ to put two pieces of wood together.

2. Use a _____ to connect two pieces of fabric.

3. Use a _____ to put two pieces of paper together.

4. Use a _____ to join two pieces of hard, thick plastic.

5. Use a _____ to fasten a map to a bulletin board.

Exercise 5 *Sentence Completion*

Write a word from the domain.

1. I need to put the pages of my homework together. Do you have a
   _____ that I could use?

2. Watch out! There is a _____ in that piece of wood. If
   you step on it, it will go through your shoe!

3. A button came off my shirt. Do you have a _____? I can try to pin it to the shirt. Maybe no one will notice.

4. I want to attach a new leg to a table. I will need a _____.

5. Did you hear about what happened on the bike path? Somebody put hundreds of carpet _____ on it. Lots of bicyclists got flat tires!

6. You can pick up _____ with a magnet.

7. **Omar:** I have to attach my photo to this application form. What should I use?

   Shizuka: You can use a _____.

For Clothing

Exercise 6 *Beginning Practice*

Look at each drawing and write the name of the object.

1. _____

4. _____

2. _____

5. _____

3. _____

Exercise 7 *Sentence Completion*

Choose the word that best completes each sentence. Write it in the blank.

The clothing industry is currently trying to make better clothes for people with physical handicaps or disabilities.

It can take a long time for disabled people to get dressed. It isn't easy for them to fasten the b_____ on their shirts. Sometimes, a shirt with
                                            1
s_____ is easier. It is also easier to use a simple metal pull on a
        2
z_____ .
        3

Belts are another problem. Belts with b_____ aren't easy to fas-
                                                    4
ten. One of the best clothes fasteners for people who have trouble with

b_____, s_____, and b_____ is
        5   6   7
v_____. It works like magic!
        8

> **buttons**
> **snaps**
> **buckles**
> **zipper**
> **velcro**

Exercise 8 *Discussion or Writing*

In a small group, quickly describe the fasteners on the clothing you are wearing. Which person in the group is wearing clothes that have the largest number of fasteners from this domain?

Sticky Fasteners

Exercise 9 *Beginning Practice*

Put the letters in the correct order to make a word from the domain.

1. reburb tmenec _____

2. stepa _____

3. gasmink peat _____

4. apte _____

5. legu _____

Exercise 10 *For Discussion and Writing*

Work in a group to answer these questions. Write down your answers.

1. What are two ways that you can use glue in your house?

2. How many different kinds of tape are there?

3. How long does it take rubber cement to dry?

4. Children in school often use paste to put things together. Did you use paste to make something in school? What was it?

For Tying

Exercise 11 *Beginning Practice*

Write the best word from the domain.

1. I need to send a package to my country. I will tie it with

   s_____g.

2. This is a birthday present for my brother. I will use blue paper to wrap it, and I will tie it with a red r_____.

3. Use that heavy l_____ to tie the sailboat to the dock.

4. He's carrying a lot of wood in the back of his truck. He should use a heavy c_____e to tie it down.

5. The zipper on my suitcase is broken. Maybe I can use a wide leather s_____p to keep it closed.

6. People who go mountain climbing need a very strong

   r_____.

7. This is a beautiful dress. Instead of a belt, it has a silk c_____d around the waist.

Exercise 12 *For Discussion or Writing*

In a group, discuss how many different things you can use to tie or connect these objects. Your teacher may ask you to write your answers.

1. to tie a boat to the dock: _____

2. to send a package to your country: _____

3. to decorate a birthday present: _____

4. to attach a large suitcase to the top of your car: _____

_____

Using What You Have Learned

The following exercises use all the words from this chapter.

Exercise 13 *Rhyming Words*

Write down a word from the domain that rhymes with the word in italics.

1. My favorite cup is broken.

What should I *do?*

Maybe you should go

and get some _____.

2. You can use a _____

to hold on your *cap.*

3. I've never seen an *ape*

that knew how to use _____.

4. Which present did he *bring?*

Is it the one with _____?

5. It wasn't very easy to carry the *table.*

We attached it to the car with some heavy _____.

6. School children sometimes put their fingers in _____,

Then they lick them so they can have a *taste!*

7. One day I was very, very *bored,*

so I used some silk to make a _____.

Exercise 14 Crossword Puzzle

Read the clues and write the correct letters in the boxes.

Answers are on page 88.

Across Clues

2. When people recycle newspapers, they can use _____ to tie them together.

5. It's made of metal and you can use it to put two pieces of paper together. It's a _____.

7. When you climb a mountain, you need a good, strong _____.

8. You find this on your belt and sometimes on your shoes. It's a _____.

Down Clues

1. A backpack is easy to open and close because it has a _____.

3. A birthday present looks pretty with a _____ on it.

4. Builders use a hammer and a _____ to join two pieces of wood.

6. Put the two pieces together or pull them apart. It's very easy to use _____.

GRAMMAR GUIDE
Count and Noncount Nouns

Look back at the words in the domain. Some of them are count nouns. Count nouns have singular and plural forms: one nail, two nails. Which words in this domain are count nouns? Which words are noncount nouns?

Exercise 15 *Reading*

Read the passage. Underline all the count nouns. Circle the noncount nouns.

I work in a busy office. My desk is covered with paper. I use a lot of paper clips, and my stapler has lots of staples in it. I also have plenty of tacks. I use them to put messages on my bulletin board. Once I dropped a tack on my boss's chair. He was not happy about that when he sat down!

Of course, I am always prepared for an emergency. I keep nails and a hammer in my desk, in case anything breaks. I have safety pins and straight pins in case my clothes tear. And I keep some thread and buttons. Everybody comes to me when they need a button or a safety pin. The people in our office always want to look their best.

My friend, Roger, works in my office too. He sends a lot of information to people. He uses glue, paste, and rubber cement to make sure the packages and letters are closed. His desk is full of different kinds of string that he uses to tie packages. When our clients receive one of his packages, it takes them a long time to open it. Roger is famous for the mail that he sends.

Focus on Noncount Words

We use special nouns to tell how much of something we need. Look at these examples:

When Roger needs more string for his office, he asks Kenji. Kenji is the person who orders office supplies.

Roger: Kenji, I need some more string.

  Kenji: How much string do you need?

Roger: Oh, two **balls** of string. That ought to be enough for this week.

Kenji has to plan his supply orders carefully. This month, he is ordering twenty-five **rolls** of tape, ten **bottles** of rubber cement, and ten **tubes** of glue. Will that be enough for this month? He isn't sure. Roger really uses a lot. Everytime Kenji looks in Roger's office, he sees **pieces** of tape and string, and **drops** of glue everywhere!

Exercise 16 *Sentence Completion*

Write the best word in the blank.

Example: I need two _____*pieces*_____ of string.

	balls
	drops
	pieces
	tubes
	rolls

1. This glue is very strong. Use only three _____.

2. How much glue does a high-school art class use in one semester?
    I think they use about twenty _____ of glue.

3. You can use as much tape as you need. We have ten
    _____ of it.

4. How much ribbon do I need to tie all these presents? I think I need two _____ of ribbon.

5. Do you have any string? I need four _____ of it.

Exercise 17 *Completion*

Write the best words from the domain in each column.

1. a drop of _____

_____

_____

3. a piece of _____

_____

_____

2. a ball of _____

_____

_____

4. a roll of _____

_____

_____

Exercise 18 *Much or Many?*

Write the correct word in the blank.

Examples: We don't have _____*much*_____ tape.

How _____*many*_____ rolls of tape do you have?

1. How _____ balls of string are there in the supply cabinet?

2. How _____ rope do you need?

3. How _____ glue will I need for this broken dish?

4. How _____ rolls of masking tape did you use?

5. How _____ rubber cement did you spill on the carpet?

Here is a domain that you already know! Many of the nouns in Domain Two are also verbs.

DOMAIN 3
Related Verbs

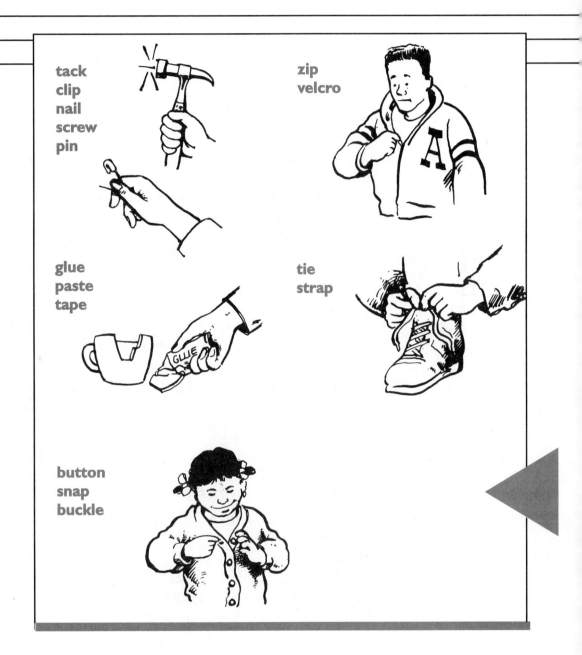

tack
clip
nail
screw
pin

zip
velcro

glue
paste
tape

tie
strap

button
snap
buckle

Exercise 19 *Describe the Action*

All of the verbs in this domain are actions. Work with a partner. Show some of these actions without using words. Your partner will guess the verb. This is called *pantomime*. Take turns showing the actions.

EXPLORING THE DOMAIN

Jaqueline Hurston is an artist. She has a big studio with a little bit of everything in it. There are metal sheets, clay, big pieces of fabric, several different kinds of paper, small piles of stones, and some colored sand. She also uses oils and watercolors.

This month, she is working on a big sculpture for a downtown office. The office owners asked for something that looks peaceful. She decided to make a garden. She drew a picture of her idea and **clipped** it to an easel. At this time, she is making flowers out of metal. She **nails** them to long pieces of wood. She will **screw** these pieces into the floor. Then she will **glue** some red, purple, and green cloth to the metal. The fabric makes the metal pieces look like soft flowers and leaves. Some of the flowers have zippers. People who see this artwork can **zip** the petals together.

She is making a big kite that she will hang from the ceiling. She will **pin** the pieces of cloth together and sew them. She will also **string** some lights across the whole sculpture.

She makes her own bricks out of clay. She will **cement** them together to make a wall around the garden. She will also **strap** some wooden birds to the ceiling. She is even going to **tack** small plastic insects to the metal leaves of the flowers.

There will be a funny scarecrow in the center of the garden. Jacqueline will make a white shirt for him and **button** it with silver nickles. She will **tie** his waist with a heavy rope. This scarecrow will have shoes that **buckle** with silver buckles. He will have a straw hat that **snaps** to his head. She is going to **velcro** his arms to his body.

When Jacqueline works on a large piece of art, she **tapes** numbers to the different parts of it. This helps her remember where each piece goes.

She is having fun working on this art project. She hopes that people will enjoy looking at it.

Exercise 20 *Sentence Completion*

Write the best word in the blank.

1. My mother always said, "Please, _____ the top of your rain-coat. I don't want you to catch a cold!"

   cement   **tack**   **snap**   **tape**

2. Don't _____ your belt too tightly! We are going to have a big barbecue supper!

   buckle   **screw**   **zip**   **paste**

3. Maria is good at sewing. She always _____ two pieces of cloth together carefully before she sews them.

   ropes   **pins**   **nails**   **straps**

4. Carlos wants all of the students to know about the talent show. He will _____ some advertisements about it on the walls of the classrooms.

   tie   **clip**   **nail**   **tape**

5. These papers are all loose. Do you have something to _____ them together?

   button   **paste**   **clip**   **velcro**

Exercise 21 *Opposites*

Many of the words in this domain have opposites. They are formed by adding *un-* to the beginning of the word. Show one of the actions below. Other students can guess what the action is.

unpin	unsnap	unbutton	unstrap
unclip	untie	unglue	

Exercise 22 *Sense or Nonsense*

Circle **Sense** if the sentence makes sense. Circle **Nonsense** if the sentence doesn't make sense.

1. Margaret doesn't know how to swim. We should throw her some string. If she holds on to it, we can pull her to the side of the pool.   **Sense**   **Nonsense**

2. Sometimes, if you don't have a screwdriver, you can use a dime to screw in a screw.   **Sense**   **Nonsense**

3. Small children like shoes that fasten with velcro. They don't have to tie anything.   **Sense**   **Nonsense**

4. You can zip two sleeping bags together to make one large sleeping bag.   **Sense**   **Nonsense**

5. A part of the right wing fell off the airplane. The pilot made an emergency landing. They taped the wing back on.   **Sense**   **Nonsense**

6. He used a strap to tie the extra boxes to his car.   **Sense**   **Nonsense**

7. What a pretty package! I will nail a bow on it.   **Sense**   **Nonsense**

8. I'm going to tack the carpet down.   **Sense**   **Nonsense**

9. The muffler fell off of my car. I hope the repairman can glue it on again.   **Sense**   **Nonsense**

10. This poster fell off the wall. I'll tie it back on again.   **Sense**   **Nonsense**

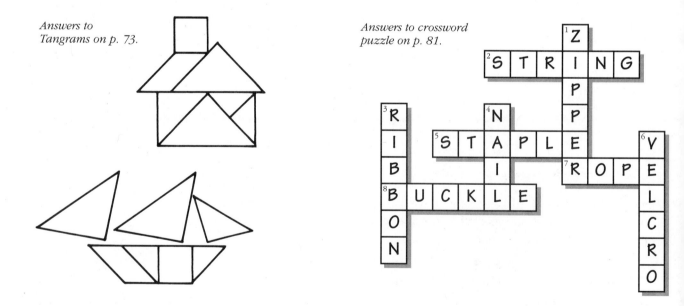

Answers to Tangrams on p. 73.

Answers to crossword puzzle on p. 81.

Chapter 9
If It Isn't Broken, Don't Fix It!

GETTING READY: Domain 1

1. What happens to a car when it hits a tree?

2. What happens to the driver?

DOMAIN 1

Break

BREAK

crack	break break into pieces come apart fall apart	crush smash
chip break off	fall to pieces	burst rupture
	shatter	

EXPLORING THE DOMAIN

Things **break**. We don't like it, but it happens. Glass **shatters**, plates **crack**, and chairs **fall apart**.

If a car hits a tree, several parts of the car and the tree might **break**. The driver might also be hurt. This is why car makers test their cars. They want to know what will happen when a car **smashes** into a concrete wall. They want to know when the engine will **crack**. They want to make sure that the glass in the windshield doesn't **shatter**. That's why cars have "safety glass". A sheet of plastic is put between two sheets of glass. The glass might **shatter**, but it doesn't **fall apart**.

Researchers test the tires too. They want to see when the tires **burst** in an accident. They also worry about the engine and the fuel tank. If the fuel tank **ruptures** easily, it can cause a dangerous fire.

Car makers use crash-test dummies. Dummies are human-size dolls that are made of plastic and rubber. These dummies **come apart** easily. Researchers can learn what happens to real people in an accident when the dummies **come apart**.

Researchers carefully study the crash-test dummies. That's why cars have airbags now. Airbags protect drivers so that the steering wheel won't **crush** them in an accident. Because of airbags, drivers also won't **chip** their teeth on the steering wheel. Car makers don't want you or your car to **fall to pieces** if you have an accident!

Exercise 1 *Beginning Practice*

Write the correct word from the domain.

Example: ocem prata _____*come apart*_____

1. srubt _____
2. akber _____
3. racck _____
4. shretta _____

5. sruch _____
6. icph _____
7. utrepru _____

Exercise 2 *Matching*

Match the action with the result.

1. I _____ my glasses.

2. I _____ a plate.

3. I _____ a mirror.

4. I _____ my hat.

5. I _____ my balloon.

6. I _____ my finger.

Exercise 3 *What Happens?*

A. Read these sentences. Write the best word in the blank.

Example: Sometimes, when a baseball hits a window, it ___cracks___ the window, but doesn't break it into pieces.

> **ruptures** **cracks** **comes apart**

1. If you drop a mirror, it will break into many small pieces. It _____.

> **shatters** **chips** **crushes**

2. There are special machines that _____ metal. These machines change the shape of the metal. For example, they take metal cans and make them flat.

> **rupture** **break** **crush**

3. This is very hard candy. I'm afraid it will break off a small piece of my tooth. Please give me some ice cream. It won't _____ a tooth.

> **burst** **chip** **smash**

4. When a helium balloon _____ and falls into the ocean it can be dangerous for sea animals. They think it is food and swallow it.

cracks   **shatters**   **bursts**

5. Appendicitis is a disease of the appendix. The appendix is an organ inside the human body. It can break open because of this disease. Appendicitis can cause an appendix to _____.

rupture   **crush**   **chip**

6. If you sit on a cardboard box, you will change its shape. The weight of your body will _____ it.

crack   **burst**   **crush**

7. Do you know the story about Goldilocks and the Three Bears? She went into the Bears' house and sat on the baby bear's chair. It _____ . The Bears came home and found the chair in pieces on the floor.

chipped   **crushed**   **fell to pieces**

8. The engineers are worried about the old bridge. There are small lines in the concrete supports. The engineers are afraid that the bridge supports are going to _____.

crack   **burst**   **shatter**

B. Choose the best word from the domain and write it in the blank. Remember to make sure that the subject and the verb agree.

1. If you put a very hot liquid into a cold glass, the glass will
   _____.

2. If you stick a pin in a balloon, the balloon will _____.

3. It is easy to _____ an aluminum can with your hand.

4. Don't ski down that long mountain. You will _____ your leg!

5. Glass usually _____ if you hit it with a stone, but safety glass doesn't.

6. When the weather gets very cold, old water pipes _____.

7. Libraries usually don't let people touch very old books. They are afraid that the books will _____.

8. If you drive at breakneck speed *(very fast)* you might really _____ your neck!

Exercise 4 *For Discussion or Writing*

Tell a story about an accident you saw. Use some of the words from this domain.

GETTING READY Domain 2

1. If a car is in an accident, it is **not working.** Can you think of some other words that mean **not working?**

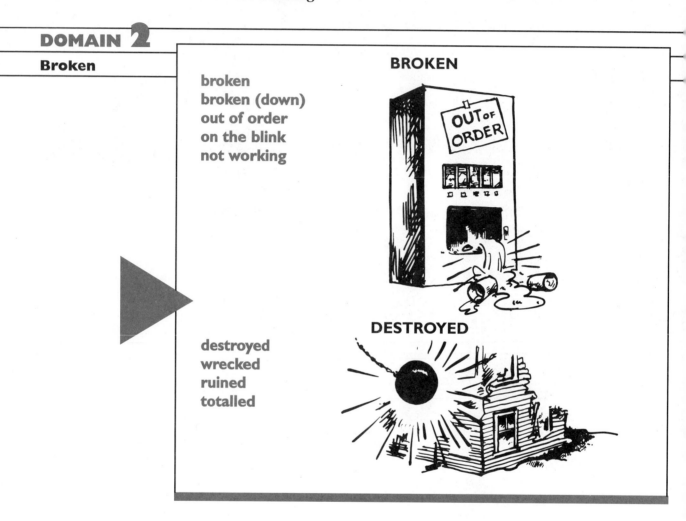

broken
broken (down)
out of order
on the blink
not working

BROKEN

OUT OF ORDER

destroyed
wrecked
ruined
totalled

DESTROYED

EXPLORING THE DOMAIN

Everything breaks eventually including cars. When a car is **on the blink**, it sometimes makes a funny sound. The owner can drive it, but it doesn't work well. A **broken down** car doesn't work at all. The owner can't drive it anywhere.

Sometimes, a mechanic can fix a car that is **not working** and make it work again. If the air-conditioner of the car is **out of order**, the mechanic will try to fix it or order a new one.

Small problems with **broken down** things are usually easy to fix. However, it is almost impossible to fix a car that is **wrecked** or **destroyed** in a bad accident. The car is **ruined**. The owner will have to get rid of the **totalled** car and buy another car. Some people take their **totalled** cars to junkyards. These cars are **not working**, but other people can still find parts that they can use.

Exercise 5 *Beginning Practice*

If something is broken, you can try to fix it. When something is destroyed, you can't really fix it. Write the rest of the words or phrases from this domain under the correct word.

totalled   out of order   wrecked   ruined

on the blink   not working   broken down

BROKEN

1. _____
2. _____
3. _____
4. _____

DESTROYED

1. _____
2. _____
3. _____

Exercise 6 *Fill in the Blank*

Write different words or phrases from the domain in the blanks.

Example: My telephone is _____ not working _____. I can't make any calls.
I'll go to my neighbor's house and call the phone company.

1. My watch is _____. Can you fix it?

2. Why did you use the vacuum cleaner to suck up water on the kitchen floor? Now, it's _____.

3. Nobody can eat this cake. It is completely burned! We'll have to throw it away because it's _____.

4. The vending machine in this building is _____ You'll have to go the cafeteria if you want a snack to munch on.

5. My computer is _____. It only saves some of my data.

6. Someone stole Antonio's car last night. The police found it this morning. All the glass was shattered, the steering wheel was cracked, and the seats were falling apart. The police officer said, "You'll never drive this car again! It's _____."

Exercise 7 *Matching*

Match each broken or destroyed object with an action.

_____	**1.** a broken window	**a.** Buy a new tire tube.
_____	**2.** a bicycle with a flat tire	**b.** Take it to the junkyard.
_____	**3.** an out of order restroom	**c.** Buy a new battery.
_____	**4.** ruined fabric on a couch	**d.** Build a new one.
_____	**5.** a TV that is on the blink	**e.** Call the plumber.
_____	**6.** a totalled car	**f.** Fix the antenna.
_____	**7.** a calculator that isn't working	**g.** Buy new glass
_____	**8.** a house that is destroyed by fire	**h.** Put a new cover on it.

Exercise 8 *For Writing or Discussion*

Answer these questions.

1. What are some things that you throw away if they are broken? Why?

2. What are some things that you keep, even if they are not working? Why?

3. What are some things that you try to fix if they are out of order? Why?

4

All About People

his unit is about *people*. We have many ways to describe people. We can describe how they look, how they think, and how they feel.

CHAPTER 10
Looking Good and Feeling Good

GETTING READY Domain 1

1. Bring in pictures from a magazine of people in advertisements.

2. What do these people look like? Why do you think magazines prefer these people for their advertisements?

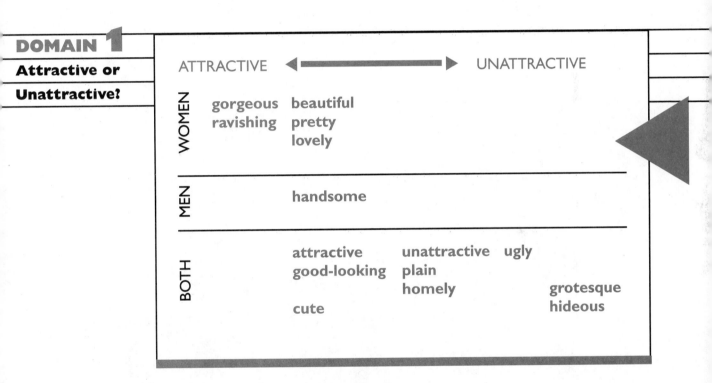

DOMAIN 1

Attractive or Unattractive?

	ATTRACTIVE ◀━━━━━▶ UNATTRACTIVE		
WOMEN	gorgeous beautiful ravishing pretty lovely		
MEN	handsome		
BOTH	attractive unattractive ugly good-looking plain homely grotesque cute hideous		

EXPLORING THE DOMAIN

Jackson Drew works in Hollywood. He is a casting director. His job is to find actors and actresses to be in movies. He has to find the right people for each movie. Last week he began to work on a new movie, "Run to Chicago."

He knows that audiences like to watch **attractive** people on the screen. So he often chooses **handsome** actors and **beautiful** actresses for his movies. One character in "Run to Chicago" is a very **good-looking** college student. For this part, Jackson has to find an actress who is more than **pretty**. She must be **gorgeous.**

Another character in the movie is a ten-year-old girl. Jackson hopes to find a **cute** young actress to play this part. For the role of the girl's mother, he is looking for a **lovely** woman who is about 35 or 40 years old.

Because there are also **unattractive** people in this world, Jackson sometimes has to look for actors or actresses who are **plain** or even **homely**. One character in "Run to Chicago" is the owner of a vending machine company. He is an **ugly** man with small eyes, bushy eyebrows, and a big nose.

Last year Jackson had to find an actor to play the part of a **grotesque**, evil person. He found a **handsome** actor who used a lot of makeup to make himself look **hideous.**

When Jackson finishes his work, the director will begin to film "Run to Chicago."

Exercise 1 *Beginning Practice*

Cross out the word that doesn't belong.

Example: beautiful ~~plain~~ attractive

1. cute good-looking homely

2. lovely ugly unattractive

3. gorgeous grotesque attractive

4. handsome homely hideous

5. ravishing pretty plain

Exercise 2 *Reproducing the Domain*

Fill in the domain chart by putting the words below in their correct places.
Ugly has been done for you.

grotesque ugly hideous gorgeous attractive

handsome pretty cute lovely

ravishing beautiful plain

good-looking homely unattractive

ATTRACTIVE ◄━━━━━━━━━━━━━━━► UNATTRACTIVE

Women

_____(1) _____(3)

_____(2) _____(4)

_____(5)

Men

_____(6)

Both

_____(7) _____(10) _____ugly_____

_____(8) _____(11)

_____(12) _____(13)

_____(9) _____(14)

Exercise 3 *Word Choice*

Complete each sentence with a word from the domain.

1. Another word for *pretty* is _____.

2. The opposite of *lovely* is _____.

3. Another word for *plain* is _____.

4. The opposite of *grotesque* is _____.

5. The word to describe an attractive man is _____.

6. Another word for *hideous* is _____.

7. One word to describe a very beautiful woman is

_____.

Exercise 4 *Sense - Nonsense*

Circle **Sense** if the sentence makes sense. Circle **Nonsense** if the sentence doesn't make sense.

1. I watched a horror movie on TV last night. One character was hideous. I closed my eyes. I didn't want to look at him.

Sense   **Nonsense**

2. It is easy to find pictures of plain women in advertisements.

Sense   **Nonsense**

3. This room is ugly. Let's paint it a different color.

Sense   **Nonsense**

4. You look ravishing in that dress. Don't buy it!

Sense   **Nonsense**

5. It's a lovely day today. Let's stay inside all day.

Sense   **Nonsense**

6. A handsome man is not a good worker.

Sense   **Nonsense**

Exercise 5 *For Discussion*

Make a list of 5 famous movie stars or TV stars that you think your class-mates will know. Then, in a small group, talk about these stars. Are they attractive or unattractive? Use as many words from the domain as possible in your discussion.

Exercise 6 *On Your Own*

There are many informal words and expressions for an attractive or unat-tractive person. They are used most often by young people. They change very quickly. Currently, a handsome man is called *a hunk*. An attractive person can be called *a fox*.

Interview some native speakers of English or watch a movie or TV show. Find some informal words to add to this domain. Share your new words with your classmates.

GETTING READY Domain 2

1. Ernesto is 5 feet 10 inches tall (1.75 meters) and weighs 250 pounds (112 kilos). Is he fat or thin?

2. In your country, how do people feel about being fat or thin?

DOMAIN 2
Underweight
or Overweight?

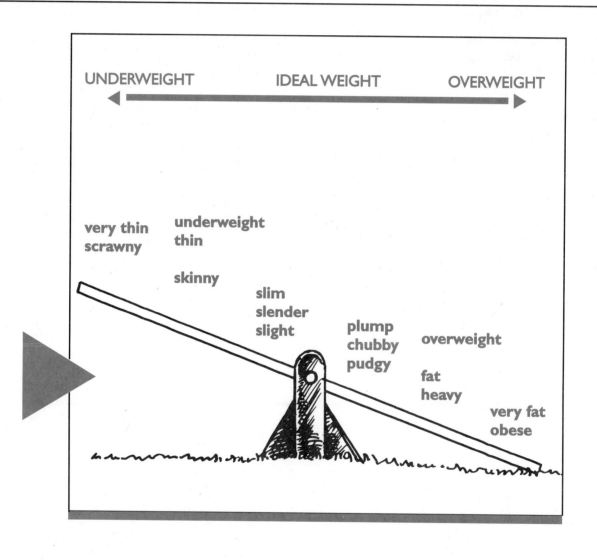

UNDERWEIGHT   IDEAL WEIGHT   OVERWEIGHT

very thin   underweight
scrawny   thin

              skinny

                   slim
                   slender
                   slight

                        plump   overweight
                        chubby
                        pudgy   fat
                                   heavy

                                        very fat
                                        obese

EXPLORING THE DOMAIN

In the United States, most people would like to be **thin**.

Fashion models and actresses are usually **slim** and **slender**. Some people say they look **scrawny** because they are too thin. In the 1960's a young woman named Twiggy was a famous fashion model. She was 5 feet 6 inches tall (1.65 meters) but weighed only 92 pounds (41.4 kilos). Many people believed she was too **skinny**.

Paintings and sculptures from decades and centuries ago show people of many different weights. The Venus of Willendorf is a small sculpture of a woman. This statue was made in Austria sometime between 15,000 and 10,000 B.C. It represents a woman who is **very fat**. It is a symbol of fertility.

Peter Paul Rubens, a Flemish painter who lived from 1577 to 1640, painted **plump** women and **chubby** children. He seemed to like people who were a little **pudgy**.

The Venus de Milo is a beautiful Greek statue. It is made of marble and represents Venus, or Aphrodite (the goddess of love and beauty). It is now in the Louvre Museum in Paris, France. A doctor might say this lovely woman is at her ideal weight. She is not **fat** and not **thin**.

Exercise 7 *Beginning Practice*

Look at the beginning and ending letters of these words from the domain.
Write the complete word in the blank.

1. h __ __ __ y   _____

2. s k __ __ __ y   _____

3. c __ __ __ __ y   _____

4. s __ __ __ __ t   _____

5. s __ __ m   _____

6. o __ __ __ e   _____

Exercise 8 *More Beginning Practice*

Arrange the words in order from underweight to overweight.

UNDERWEIGHT ══════════════▶ OVERWEIGHT

1. thin   fat   obese   pudgy

_____   _____   _____   _____

2. heavy   slender   chubby   skinny

_____   _____   _____   _____

3. slim   obese   scrawny   plump

_____   _____   _____   _____

Exercise 9 *Word Choice*

Choose a word from the domain that you think describes the person in
each sentence.

1. Sam hates vegetables and never eats fruit. He loves potato chips,
chocolate, fried foods, and steaks. Every day he gulps down three
big meals and three or four snacks. His doctor is worried about his
health.

Sam is probably _____.

2. Carlos has been sick for four months. He has been eating like a bird.

Carlos is probably _____.

3. Linda doesn't like sweet food. She eats a lot of salads made with fresh vegetables and a lot of fruit.

Linda is probably _____.

4. Everyday for lunch Jason pigs out on three hamburgers and a piece of pizza. Then he eats some ice cream.

Jason is probably _____.

5. Ana is fifteen years old. She thinks she is too fat. She doesn't want to gain weight. She picks at her food, and she often skips one or two meals a day. Her doctor says she is not fat. He is worried about her.

Ana is probably _____.

Exercise 10 *For Discussion*

The words in the list are from Domain 1. Choose the word that you think describes each person. Discuss your answers with your classmates.

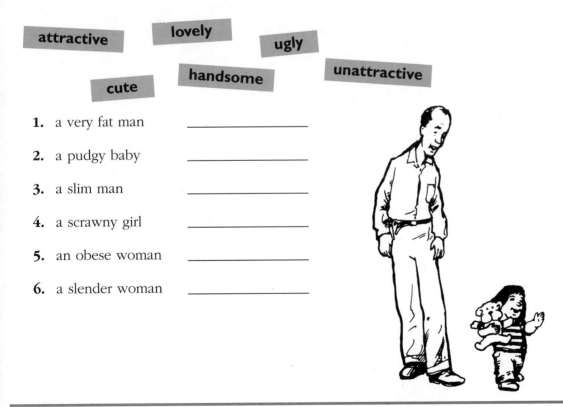

attractive   lovely   ugly   cute   handsome   unattractive

1. a very fat man   _____

2. a pudgy baby   _____

3. a slim man   _____

4. a scrawny girl   _____

5. an obese woman   _____

6. a slender woman   _____

Exercise 11 *For Writing or Discussion*

1. Reubens liked pudgy women. Currently, in many countries, the ideal woman is thin. Is this true in your country? What do people think about a woman who is heavy? Will her weight affect her chances for success?

2. What about men? What is the ideal weight for a man? What do people think about a heavy man? Will his weight affect his chances for success?

Exercise 12 *For Writing*

Imagine that you are stuck in an elevator with four other people. Write one or two sentences to describe each of the people in the elevator. Use as many words from Domains 1 and 2 as you can.

GETTING READY Domain 3

1. Have you ever been really sick? How did you feel?

2. How did you feel when you got out of bed this morning? Did you feel good or bad?

All the words and phrases in this domain can be used to answer the question, "How do you feel?"

DOMAIN 3

Sick or Well?

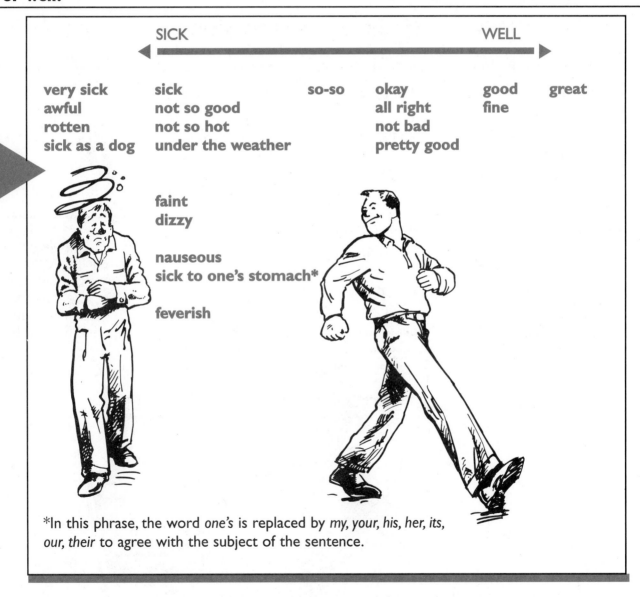

SICK ← → WELL

very sick	sick	so-so	okay	good	great
awful	not so good		all right	fine	
rotten	not so hot		not bad		
sick as a dog	under the weather		pretty good		

faint
dizzy

nauseous
sick to one's stomach*

feverish

*In this phrase, the word *one's* is replaced by *my, your, his, her, its, our, their* to agree with the subject of the sentence.

EXPLORING THE DOMAIN

Kevin and his friend Takuji had the following conversations last week.

TUESDAY

Takuji: Shinji and I are going to a movie tonight. Do you want to go with us, Kevin?

Kevin: Thanks, but I think I'll stay home. I **don't feel so hot**. I feel **faint** and **sick to my stomach.** I'm going to go to bed early.

WEDNESDAY

Takuji: We missed you at the movie last night, Kevin. Are you still **under the weather**?

Kevin: Now I feel even worse. In fact, I'm **sick as a dog**. I hurt all over.

Takuji: I think you should call the doctor. This sounds serious.

Kevin: Yeah. I feel **awful**. If I don't feel better this afternoon, I'll call Dr. Huang.

Takuji: Let me know if you need a ride to his office. You sound too sick to drive.

THURSDAY

Kevin: Thanks for the ride to the doctor yesterday, Takuji.

Takuji: Don't mention it. How do you feel today?

Kevin: **So-so.** When the nurse took my temperature yesterday, it was 102˚. I don't feel as **feverish** today. My temperature is down to 99˚. I think I'll be **all right** by tomorrow.

Takuji: Well, take it easy. You had a bad case of the flu and you need to rest.

FLU: *(influenza)* a contagious disease whose symptoms include muscle pain, headache, nausea, and often, a high fever.

YOU HAVE THE FLU.

FRIDAY

Takuji: Hey Kevin, how are you doing?

Kevin: **Great**! I feel much better than I did yesterday. I think I'll be able to go to that party with you tomorrow night.

Takuji: I don't know. I **don't feel so good** myself.

Kevin: Oh, no! Well, if you get the flu, I'll be glad to drive you to the doctor's office!

Exercise 13 *Beginning Practice*

Put the words in order from sick to well.

SICK ━━━━━━━━━━━━━━━━━━━━━━━━━━▶ WELL

1. so-so   fine   rotten

_____ _____ _____

2. pretty good   not so good   great

_____ _____ _____

3. good   sick as a dog   not bad   not so hot

_____ _____ _____ _____

4. all right   awful   under the weather   so-so   great

_____ _____ _____ _____ _____

Exercise 14 *More Beginning Practice*

Complete each sentence with a word from the domain.

1. Another word for *sick* is _____.

2. Another word for *faint* is _____.

3. The opposite of *sick as a dog* is _____.

4. If Harry is sick to his stomach, he is _____.

5. If you feel just a little sick, you feel _____.

6. If you feel just a little better than so-so, you feel _____.

Exercise 15 *Word Choice*

Complete the sentence with a word from the list.

1. Laura's skin is very hot. How does she feel?

   She feels _____.

2. Collin's head hurts and he is nauseous. How does he feel?

   He feels _____.

3. Last week Andy was in the hospital for two days. Now he is at home. His doctor told him to stay in bed for one more day. How does he feel?

   He feels _____.

4. George slept for 8 hours last night. This morning he woke up early. He jumped out of bed and got ready to play basketball with his friends. How does he feel?

   He feels _____.

Exercise 16 *Pair Work*

Do this exercise with a partner. First read the dialogues below. Then write two short dialogues of your own. Be prepared to present your dialogues to the rest of the class.

Dialogue I.

Student A: How do you feel today?

Student B: Pretty good! My cold is much better now.

Dialogue II.

Student A: Why didn't you come to class yesterday?

Student B: I felt rotten. I think I ate some bad food.

Student A: Were you sick to your stomach?

Student B: Yes, and I felt faint, too.

Exercise 17 *For Discussion*

Make a list of words in your language that mean 'sick' and 'well'. Compare them to the words in this domain in English. Which language has more words for *sick?* For *well?* Do you have words for *very sick, sick,* and *so-so* in your language*?*

Exercise 18 *For Writing*

Think of an illness or injury that you had. Maybe it was a bad cold, an infection, or a broken leg. Describe how you felt when you had that illness or injury. You may want to use a bilingual dictionary to look up words that describe how you felt. For example, in the dialogue on page 110, Kevin had the flu. He said that he felt faint and that he hurt all over. Write a short paragraph describing how you felt when you were ill or injured.

CHAPTER 11
On the Inside

GETTING READY Domain 1

Chapter 10 teaches many words that describe physical characteristics of people (attractive - unattractive, fat - thin, sick - well). We can easily see these characteristics the first time we meet someone.

People have other characteristics that we can't see. For example, they can be smart or nice. Work in a small group to name as many of these other characteristics as you can. Then share your list with the class.

DOMAIN 1

Intelligent or
Unintelligent?

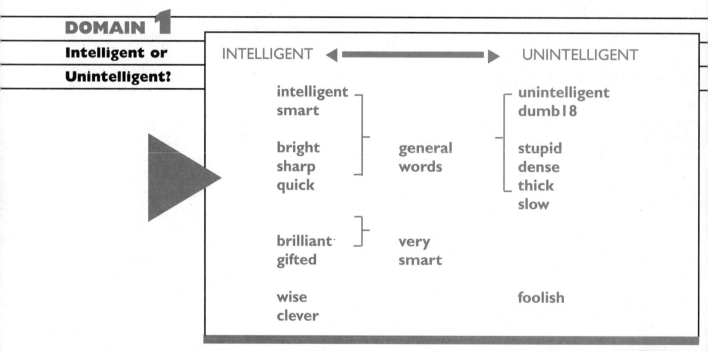

INTELLIGENT ◀━━━━━━▶ UNINTELLIGENT

intelligent
smart

bright
sharp   general
quick   words

brilliant
gifted   very
               smart

wise
clever

unintelligent
dumb18

stupid
dense
thick
slow

foolish

EXPLORING THE DOMAIN

Are animals **smart** or **dumb**? What about computers? Are they **intelligent** or **unintelligent**? If a person has a small brain, is that person **slow**? The answers to these questions might surprise you.

Washoe is a female chimpanzee. Her trainers think she is **bright**. They trained her to communicate with humans using sign language, the language used by deaf people. She can *talk* by using 130 signs. Her trainers say she is **clever** enough to create new signs.

On the other hand, people who work with computers say that some of today's machines are **stupid**. The current generation of computers cannot think. They cannot make **brilliant** decisions by themselves. But computer scientists are working on new computers that use artificial intelligence. These computers won't be as **dense** as those we use now. They will be able to think more like the human brain. Today we say that a person who is **intelligent** and knows many things is **wise**. Someday soon we may talk about those **wise** computers!

A university professor in England discovered that brain size is not related to intelligence. He examined a student who had a very small brain. He expected this student to be **slow** and **thick**. But the student was actually **sharp** and **quick**. Tests showed that he had an IQ of 126, which is more than average. He wasn't **brilliant**, but he was more than **smart**. The professor found several hundred people who have very small brains but are **intelligent**.

Exercise 1 *Beginning Practice*

Put an **I** next to the words that mean 'intelligent'. Put a **U** next to the words that mean 'unintelligent'. *Dense* has been done for you.

1. _U_ dense	**5.** ___ stupid	**9.** ___ wise	**12.** ___ clever
2. ___ sharp	**6.** ___ quick	**10.** ___ smart	**13.** ___ dumb
3. ___ slow	**7.** ___ brilliant	**11.** ___ foolish	**14.** ___ thick
4. ___ gifted	**8.** ___ bright		

Exercise 2 *More Beginning Practice*

Put a letter in each blank to complete a word from the domain. The letters in the boxes will spell the name of a gifted scientist.

1. __ __ ☐ __ __ __   opposite of foolish

2. __ __ ☐ __ __   dumb

3. __ __ ☐ __ __   opposite of sharp

4. __ __ __ __ __ ☐ __   not wise

5. __ __ __ __ __ ☐   quick

6. __ __ __ __ ☐ __   very smart

7. __ __ __ __ __ ☐ __ __ __   gifted

8. __ ☐ __ __ __ __ __ __ __ __   smart

Albert _____ was a brilliant scientist.

Exercise 3 *Exploring* wise, clever, *and* foolish

The words *wise, clever,* and *foolish* have special meanings.

A wise person is someone who knows many things. A wise person also knows how to use that knowledge. Older people are often wise.

A clever person uses his intelligence to do things. For example, a clever person might tell good jokes or know how to fix things or how to make a lot of money.

A foolish person does stupid or silly things. He might run across a busy street without waiting for a green light or walk in the snow with no shoes on.

A. Do you have words for *wise, clever,* and *foolish* in your language?

B. Work in a small group. Tell your classmates a story from your country about a person or an animal who is wise, clever, or foolish.

Exercise 4 *For Discussion*

A. Think of a person who has one of the qualities listed below. Write the person's name in the blank. Do this for three or more of the words. The person can be a famous person, a TV or movie character, or someone you know. Then share your answers in a small group. Give an example that shows why you chose that person.

quick _____ foolish _____

stupid _____ gifted _____

B. We think of some animals as being smart and others as being dumb. Write the name of an animal next to three or more of the words below. Be ready to discuss your answers.

smart _____ slow _____

clever _____ wise _____

dumb _____ bright _____

Exercise 5 *For Writing or Discussion*

1. What are some characteristics of an intelligent person?

2. Have you ever taken an intelligence test? What was it like? Do you think it is a good way to measure intelligence?

3. Do gifted people always do well in school? Why or why not? Do you know of a gifted person who did not do well in school?

Exercise 6 *On Your Own*

There are many informal words in English for people who are smart. A smart person can be called *a brain, a genius, a whiz*. There are also many words for people who are not smart. You will insult people if you call them *a moron* or *an idiot.*

Find as many other words as you can for smart or stupid people. You can ask native speakers or use your dictionary or a thesaurus.

GETTING READY Domain 2

1. Do you know someone who is nice? Why do you think he or she is nice?

2. Do you know someone who is not nice? What do people who are not nice do?

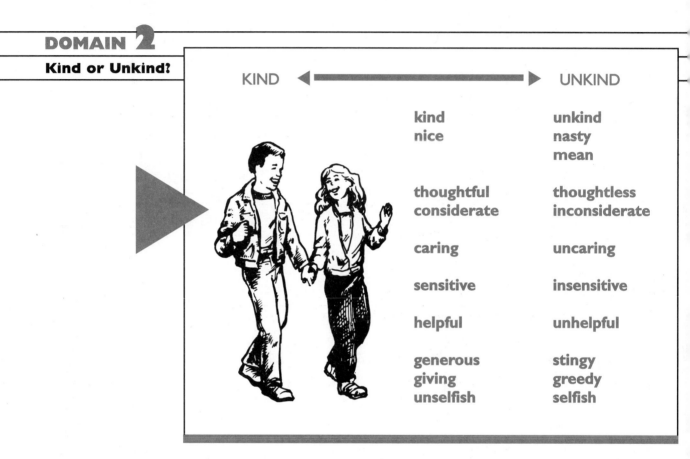

DOMAIN 2
Kind or Unkind?

KIND	UNKIND
kind	unkind
nice	nasty
	mean
thoughtful	thoughtless
considerate	inconsiderate
caring	uncaring
sensitive	insensitive
helpful	unhelpful
generous	stingy
giving	greedy
unselfish	selfish

EXPLORING THE DOMAIN

Mary Ann is 46 years old. She is married and has two children. She is a **kind**, **generous** person. One day each week she works as a volunteer at Madison House, a homeless shelter. Madison House is in a poor area of Seattle, Washington. People who have no money and no place to live can go there to eat and sleep.

Henry comes to Madison House almost every day. Sometimes Mary Ann brings him a cup of coffee and then sits across from him. She listens while he tells her about his problems. She is **considerate** to Henry and to all the people who come to Madison House.

Henry is a **nice** person, but some people who visit Madison House are **mean** and **nasty**. They complain about the food and talk loudly late at night when other people are sleeping. Some people even steal food or money from the others. But Mary Ann and the other volunteers try to be **caring** and **helpful** to everyone. They understand that life is not easy for homeless people.

Last month a new volunteer, Jason, started to work at Madison House. Mary Ann thinks Jason is **insensitive.** Last week Jason told Henry that he was lazy and dense. Both Henry and Mary Ann think that Jason will soon stop coming to Madison House. **Thoughtless** people are usually not good volunteers.

Many **kind, giving** people don't have time to work as volunteers. They often give money to Madison House and other charities.

Exercise 7 *Beginning Practice*

Put a **K** next to all the words that mean 'kind' and a **U** next to all the words that mean 'unkind'.

1. ___ insensitive   5. ___ giving   9. ___ mean

2. ___ nice   6. ___ inconsiderate   10. ___ stingy

3. ___ unselfish   7. ___ selfish   11. ___ thoughtful

4. ___ caring   8. ___ greedy   12. ___ nasty

Exercise 8 *Speaking Practice*

Work with a partner. You cover the domain. Your partner will read a word from the domain. Give a word that is opposite in meaning. Take turns reading words from the domain.

Example: Your partner says: "insensitive"
You say: "sensitive"

Exercise 9 *Word Choice*

Circle the word that best describes the person.

1. Sheila says things that make her friends feel bad. When she saw her friend Sarah for the first time in two weeks, she said, "You look fat! You've gained a lot of weight!"   **thoughtful   thoughtless**

2. Kelly always remembers to send birthday cards to her friends. **considerate   inconsiderate**

3. Bill's friend just got home from the hospital. Bill took some food and a new book to him.   **caring   uncaring**

4. Kate Wilson teaches first grade. She often doesn't notice an unhappy student.   **sensitive   insensitive**

5. Claude's grandmother broke her leg. He goes to her house every week to cut her grass.   **helpful   unhelpful**

6. Ahmed likes to go to a restaurant with his friends. But he never pays his part of the bill.   **generous   stingy**

Exercise 10 *Matching*

Match the person with the action.

_____ 1. sends a birthday card to a friend

_____ 2. never shares; keeps everything for herself

_____ 3. brings one small bottle of soda to a potluck dinner

_____ 4. spends his day off at the hospital helping the patients

_____ 5. borrows clothes from her roommate without asking

a. a stingy person

b. an insensitive person

c. a selfish person

d. a considerate person

e. a generous person

Exercise 11 *For Discussion or Writing*

The paragraphs below describe three different people. Read each paragraph. Then decide which person you would like to have for a friend. Either in writing or orally, explain why you chose that person.

1. Ashley is a thoughtful person. She always remembers to send cards to her friends on their birthdays. She is also very helpful. When her friend moved to a new apartment, Ashley worked for ten hours to help her move. But sometimes she is a little stingy. She doesn't like to spend money. She doesn't always pay her share of the bill when she eats at a restaurant with her friends.

2. Tomas is not very handsome but he is generous and helpful. He works as a volunteer at the Student Learning Center. He helps international students learn English. Some of his friends think he is inconsiderate. Sometimes he says thoughtless things to them.

3. Angela is an attractive person but she is unkind to her friends. For example, last week she told her friend, "I'll drive you to your job interview." But she forgot to do it. She often does inconsiderate things like this. But she is generous. She bought her friend a very expensive present for her birthday.

Exercise 12 *Expanding the Domain*

A. The words in the list below mean either 'kind' or 'unkind'. Put a **K** in front of the word if you think it means *kind* and a **U** if you think it means *unkind*. You can use your dictionary or ask your classmates or a native speaker.

1. ___ soft-hearted   5. ___ hard-hearted

2. ___ heartless   6. ___ cold-hearted

3. ___ kind-hearted   7. ___ warm-hearted

4. ___ good-hearted

B. These words show that in English we use the word *heart* to talk about kindness. What word or words do you use in your language?

GETTING READY Domain 3

When you were a child, your parents tried to teach you to be a good person. What did they teach you? What characteristics does a good person have?

DOMAIN 3
Other Characteristics

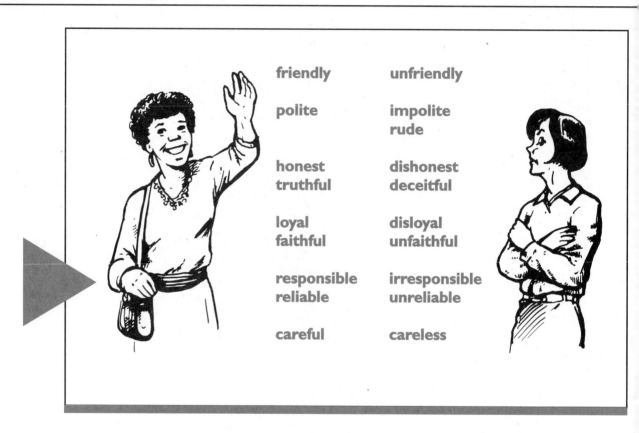

friendly	unfriendly
polite	impolite rude
honest truthful	dishonest deceitful
loyal faithful	disloyal unfaithful
responsible reliable	irresponsible unreliable
careful	careless

EXPLORING THE DOMAIN

Melissa Heston wants to become the first woman governor of Virginia. But she knows it will not be easy to win the election.

In her speeches, she tells the voters of Virginia that she is an **honest** person. She shows them that she always tells the truth. She also shows that she is **reliable**. When she says she will do something, she does it. Ms. Heston also wants the people to think that she is a **responsible** person. She will be **careful** with the money of the people of Virginia.

In one of her speeches, she might say that her opponent is **careless** with money. She might tell the voters that her opponent wasted their money. He used government planes to take vacations. She will also say he is **disloyal** to his friends. She will claim that last year he refused to help a good friend.

Melissa Heston is a **friendly** person. She says hello to everyone and likes to talk with the campaign workers during lunch. But when she has to give an important speech, she becomes a little **rude**. When she is under a lot of pressure, she can become **impolite.** In a loud, **unfriendly** voice, she tells her secretary to bring her some coffee. She is **impolite** to people on the telephone, too. But when the speech is finished, she goes back to being a nice person to work with.

Exercise 13 *Beginning Practice*

Fill in the blank with a word from the domain that is opposite in meaning.

1. truthful _____

2. careless _____

3. disloyal _____

4. honest _____

5. polite _____

6. unfriendly _____

7. faithful _____

8. responsible _____

9. unreliable _____

Exercise 14 *Speaking Practice*

Work with a partner. You cover the domain. Your partner will read a word from the domain. Give the word that is opposite in meaning. Take turns.

Example: Your partner says: "careless"
             You say: "careful"

Exercise 15 *Matching*

Choose a word from the list that best describes each person. Then write the word in the blank.

1. My niece always says "please" when she asks for something.

   _____

2. Harry tells his boss he is sick. He is really well, but he wants the day off.

   _____

3. Beth says mean things about her best friend.

   _____

4. Sara always tells her mother when she has done something wrong. She never lies to her mother.

   _____

5. Bob smiles and says "hello" as he walks down the street.

   _____

6. Judy always says she will finish her part of a report on time. But she never does.

   _____

friendly
dishonest
truthful
unreliable
polite
unfaithful

Exercise 16 *Sense or Nonsense*

Circle **Sense** if the sentence makes sense. Circle **Nonsense** if the sentence doesn't make sense.

1. Ana is an irresponsible student. She always does her homework on time.

   Sense   **Nonsense**

2. Karen is a reliable employee. She always comes to work on time and does her work carefully.

   Sense   **Nonsense**

3. Jorge is an accountant. He lost his job because he made many mistakes. He was too careful.

   Sense   **Nonsense**

4. Christina sold secrets to another country. She is a disloyal citizen.

   Sense   **Nonsense**

5. Andy always says "please" and "thank you." He never talks when someone else is talking. He is a rude child.

   Sense   **Nonsense**

6. Andre bought a pen for $.99. He gave the clerk a $5.00 bill. She gave him $9.01 in change. Andre told her about the mistake and returned $5.00 to her. He is a deceitful person.

   Sense   **Nonsense**

7. Jose has many friends. He smiles and says hello to many people as he walks around campus. He is an unfriendly person.

   Sense   **Nonsense**

8. During the election, Henry Alton promised to build a new school. After he won the election, he said the new school was too expensive. He was unfaithful to the people who voted for him.

   Sense   **Nonsense**

Exercise 17 *For Writing: Rate Yourself*

A. How would you rate yourself on the following characteristics? Circle the number that you think best describes you.

1.	friendly	**5 4 3 2 1**	unfriendly
2.	careful	**5 4 3 2 1**	careless
3.	polite	**5 4 3 2 1**	impolite
4.	responsible	**5 4 3 2 1**	irresponsible
5.	loyal	**5 4 3 2 1**	disloyal

B. Write a short paragraph about yourself. Tell which characteristic you would like to change and why.

Exercise 18 *For Discussion*

Look at the words below. Which characteristics do you think are the most important for the leader of a country to have? In a small group put the words in order from the most important to the least important for a leader to have. Share your answers with the class.

honest   polite   careful   friendly   responsible   reliable   loyal

Exercise 19 *For Writing*

1. Can you remember a time when you were rude, dishonest, careless, unfriendly, or disloyal? Write a short paragraph about what happened.

2. Write a short paragraph about a time when you were truthful, responsible, polite, reliable, or faithful.

CHAPTER 12
The World of Emotions

GETTING READY Domain 1

1. Unit 4 presents many words that describe people. Look at the titles of Chapters 10 and 11. Now look at the title of this chapter. What kinds of words do you think you will learn in this chapter?

2. How do you feel before you take a big, important test?

3. How do you feel when you are listening to beautiful music?

DOMAIN 1

Upset - Calm

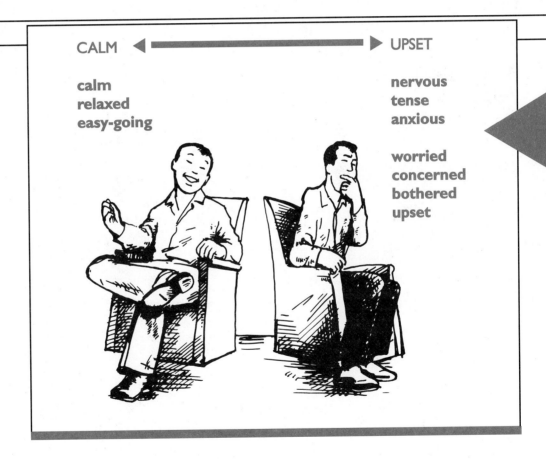

CALM ◄——————————► UPSET

calm
relaxed
easy-going

nervous
tense
anxious

worried
concerned
bothered
upset

EXPLORING THE DOMAIN

Osamu and Wakako live in Tokyo. Osamu is an **easy-going** person. He is usually **calm** and **relaxed**. His friends enjoy spending time with him because he is almost always happy. But last week Osamu changed.

Osamu: I can't go out for pizza with you tonight, Wakako. I'm too busy!

Wakako: Osamu, what's the matter with you? I invite you out for pizza, and you get all **upset**. In fact, you've been **tense** all week. I'm **worried** about you.

Osamu: I'm sorry, Wakako. I didn't mean to make you **upset**. It's just that I'm taking the TOEFL test next week, and I'm really **anxious** about it.

Wakako: What's the TOEFL test?

Osamu: It's the Test of English as a Foreign Language. I want to study in the U.S. next semester, so I have to take it.

Wakako: What will happen if you don't pass the test?

Osamu: Then I can't go to the U.S. to study.

Wakako: Oh, now I understand why you are **tense** and **worried**.

Osamu: Yeah, but don't worry. I'll be back to my old, **easy-going** self soon.

Wakako: Great! Then we can go out for pizza together.

Exercise 1 *Beginning Practice*

Fill in the blanks to complete the words. Then write the complete word in the blank.

1. <u>b</u> _ _ <u>h</u> _ _ _ <u>d</u> _____

2. <u>r</u> _ _ <u>a</u> <u>x</u> _ _ _____

3. _ <u>o</u> _ <u>c</u> _ _ <u>n</u> _ _ _____

4. <u>u</u> _ <u>s</u> _ _ _____

5. <u>a</u> _ <u>x</u> _ _ _ <u>s</u> _____

6. <u>c</u> _ _ <u>m</u> _____

Exercise 2 *More Beginning Practice*

Look at the list of words below. Put each word in the correct column.

Calm	Upset	
_____	_____	concerned
_____	_____	tense
_____	_____	worried
	_____	easy-going
	_____	nervous
	_____	calm
	_____	upset
		relaxed
		anxious
		bothered

Exercise 3 *Matching*

Match the situation with a word that describes how you would feel in that situation. Write the word in the blank.

tense   relaxed   upset   calm

A. **1.** on vacation in Hawaii _____

2. at a job interview _____

3. talking to a policeman after a car accident _____

4. walking in the woods with a good friend _____

relaxed

nervous

bothered   concerned

B. **1.** listening to music that you don't like _____

2. waiting for a family member to come home on a

stormy night   _____

3. watching a good, funny movie   _____

4. waiting to see the dentist   _____

Exercise 4 *For Writing and Discussion*

A. Write four short sentences. In two sentences describe a situation that makes you feel upset. In two sentences describe a situation that makes you feel calm.

B. Work with a partner. Read your sentences to your partner one at a time. Ask your partner how he or she would feel in the situation you described.

Exercise 5 *For Writing*

Write a short paragraph about one of the following topics:

1. What kinds of things or events make you feel nervous, concerned, or upset?

2. Tell about a time when you felt very calm and relaxed **or** very tense and anxious. Where were you? Who were you with?

3. Create a relaxing scene. Where does it take place?

4. Create a tense scene. Where does it take place?

GETTING READY Domain 2

1. Imagine that you are crossing a street. You see a car coming toward you at a high speed. How do you feel? What happens to your heart rate? Your breathing?

2. Have you ever been *really* scared? What happened to scare you so much?

AFRAID

Afraid	Very Afraid
afraid	terrified
scared	horrified
frightened	petrified
fearful	scared stiff

EXPLORING THE DOMAIN
Confessions of a Wimp

Some of my friends call me a wimp because I am **afraid** of so many things. I am **frightened** by spiders, and I feel **scared** when I walk into a dark room. I am **afraid** of meeting new people, too. I am just a **fearful** person.

Some things make me more than **frightened**. When I look down from the top of a very tall building, I am **scared stiff**. I am **horrified** by being alone. I never go to horror movies because I am **terrified** by them. When I saw "Bride of Frankenstein," I was absolutely **petrified**. I got sick to my stomach and couldn't sleep that night.

It's no fun being a wimp. I wonder if I'll ever change.

Exercise 6 *Beginning Practice*

Unscramble the letters. Write a word from the domain in the blank.

1. ffelaru _____

2. pdrifteie _____

3. rcdeas _____

4. rrieiedtf _____

5. tfrnieeghd _____

Exercise 7 *More Beginning Practice*

Fill in the blanks. When you finish, the boxes will give the name of something that can make you feel afraid.

b

1. synonym of afraid   __ __ [ ] __ __ __

2. really scared   __ __ __ __ [ ] __ __ __ __

3. too scared to move   __ __ __ __ __ __ __ [ ]

4. synonym of terrified   __ __ __ [ ] __ __ __ __

5. very, very scared   __ __ __ __ __ __ [ ] __

6. full of fear   __ __ [ ] __ __ __ __

m

s

I feel very frightened when I have _____ _____ .

Exercise 8 *Ordering*

Put the words in order using words from Domain 1 and Domain 2.

CALM ━━▶ UPSET ━━▶ AFRAID ━━▶ VERY AFRAID

| | petrified | anxious | relaxed |

Example: ___relaxed___   ___anxious___   ___petrified___

1. fearful   horrified   concerned

_____   _____   _____

2. nervous   easy-going   scared

_____   _____   _____

3. scared stiff   bothered   afraid   relaxed

_____   _____   _____   _____

4. upset   calm   terrified   frightened

_____   _____   _____   _____

Exercise 9   *How Do You Feel When....?*

Read over the situations described below. Then circle the word that best describes how you would feel in that situation. Your answers may differ from the answers of your classmates because they are your feelings.

How do you feel when....

   1.   you are in a tunnel?

   scared stiff   **tense**   **calm**   **fearful**

   2.   you are meeting new people?

   relaxed   **petrified**   **frightened**   **anxious**

   3.   you are in a crowd (a large group of people)?

   scared   **nervous**   **calm**   **terrified**

   4.   you are in a lake or an ocean?

   horrified   **relaxed**   **afraid**   **upset**

   5.   you are flying in an airplane?

   fearful   **calm**   **tense**   **terrified**

   6.   you are in a small, dark place?

   scared   **worried**   **scared stiff**   **relaxed**

Exercise 10   *Word Choice*

Read the paragraph through once. Then choose the word that best completes each sentence. Write it in the blank.

Elena was a little _____ (petrified/nervous). She was walking
                                   1
home alone late at night. Steps! She heard steps. Someone was walking
behind her. She began to feel _____ (calm/frightened). She
                                              2
walked faster. She could see her house at the end of the street. Suddenly
the steps became louder and faster. The person behind her was trying to
catch her. Elena was _____ (uneasy/terrified)! She began to run
                                    3
toward her house. Then she heard her brother's voice. "Elena, why are you
running? I just want to walk home with you." She was very happy to see
her brother. By the time they arrived home, Elena was feeling
_____(calm/scared) again.
          4

Exercise 11 *Sense or Nonsense*

Circle **Sense** if the sentence makes sense. Circle **Nonsense** if the sentence doesn't make sense.

1. I didn't prepare well for this presentation. I feel nervous about it.

   Sense   **Nonsense**

2. She rented an apartment on the 16th floor because she is scared stiff of high places.

   Sense   **Nonsense**

3. I am frightened of dogs. When I see one, I go to the other side of the street.

   Sense   **Nonsense**

4. When I see a snake, I scream and run away as fast as I can. I am uneasy about snakes.

   Sense   **Nonsense**

5. Parents feel relaxed when they watch their child cross the street alone for the first time.

   Sense   **Nonsense**

Exercise 12 *On Your Own*

A wimp is a person who is always afraid. There are many other words in English for people who are fearful. Find as many other words as you can for fearful people. You can ask native speakers or use your dictionary or a thesaurus.

Exercise 13 *For Discussion or Writing*

Tell or write a story about a time when you were frightened or terrified. Share your story in a group or with a partner.

GETTING READY Domain 3

How do you feel when:

—someone is not honest with you?

—your parents make you do something you don't want to do?

—someone parks their car in a parking space you waited 5 minutes for?

DOMAIN 3

Angry

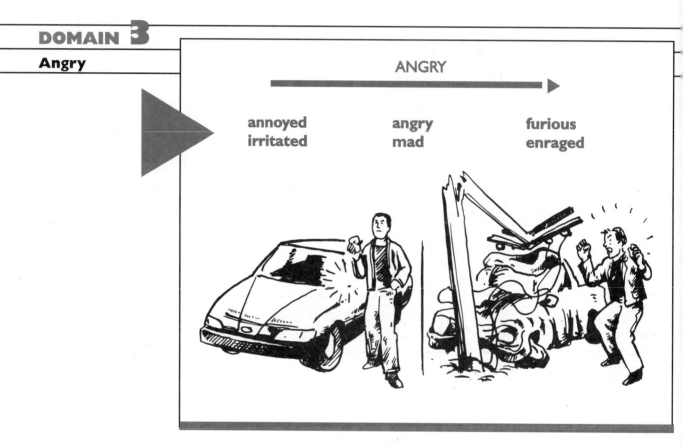

ANGRY

annoyed	angry	furious
irritated	mad	enraged

EXPLORING THE DOMAIN

Last month I bought a new car. It was bright red and sporty, and I really liked it.

On the day I bought it, I was very excited. I called my friend Stergios and asked him if he would like to go for a ride. I told him I would pick him up in ten minutes. But I couldn't find the car keys. I looked for them for a long time and finally found them. They were locked inside the car. I was **annoyed**. Locking the keys in the car is such a stupid thing to do! I called Stergios and told him the problem. He was **irritated** too. His friend had invited him to go bowling, but Stergios had turned down the invitation so he could ride in my new car.

A week later I discovered that the rear view mirror on the driver's side had fallen off. I was more than **irritated** by this. I was **angry**. I called the dealer who sold me the car. I think he knew I was **mad**. He was very nice to me. He told me to bring the car to the service center the next day and they would fix it for free. I felt more calm after I talked to him.

Last week someone stole my new car! I left my apartment early in the morning to go to work. I had my keys, but my car was gone. I was **furious**. How could someone steal my new red sports car? I called the police.

Two days later they found my car, but it was ruined. When I saw it, I became **enraged**. The thief had smashed my car into a telephone pole at a high speed. It was totalled. I was so **angry** that I couldn't speak. Fortunately I had insurance, and I will be able to buy a new car soon.

Exercise 14 *Beginning Practice*

Fill in the blanks to complete the word. Then write the complete word in the blank.

1. f __ __ __ o __ s   _____

2. __ __ d   _____

3. __ r __ __ t __ __ __ d   _____

4. e __ __ __ g __ __   _____

5. a __ __ __ y   _____

6. a __ n __ __ __ d   _____

Exercise 15 *Word Choice*

Working alone, choose the word that you think best completes the sentence. Then in a small group discuss your answers.

1. Tom's son just told him a big lie. Tom is _____.

   mad   **furious**   **irritated**

2. The person sitting next to me in the movie theater talked loudly during the whole movie. I was _____.

   annoyed   **angry**   **enraged**

3. My friend borrowed some money from me last week. He didn't pay me back. Today he asked to borrow more money. I was

_____.

furious   irritated   mad

4. I am a soccer coach. My team lost the game today. We lost because two of our best players got thrown out of the game. I was _____.

annoyed   enraged   angry

Exercise 16 *For Discussion*

When we are annoyed, angry or furious, things happen. Work in a small group. Put each item in the column where you think it belongs.

red face	**very red face**	**smash your hand through the door**
sweat	**rapid heartbeat**	**leave the room**
tap fingers	**can't sit still**	**slap the table**
scream	**talk loudly**	**refuse to continue the conversation**
slam the door		

Annoyed/Irritated	Angry/Mad	Furious/Enraged
_____	_____	_____
_____	_____	_____
_____	_____	_____
_____	_____	_____
_____	_____	_____
_____	_____	_____
_____	_____	_____
_____	_____	_____

Exercise 17 *For Discussion or Writing*

1. Make a list of four things that make you feel annoyed or irritated.

2. Do you remember a time when you were furious or enraged? What made you so angry? What did you do?

3. Some people get angry a lot. Other people almost never get mad. What kind of person are you?

4. Do you think that being angry is positive or negative? Why?

WORD LIST

The number after the word or phrase indicates the chapter.

a bite to eat	4	bright	11
a long time ago	2	brilliant	11
a short time ago	2	broil	6
about	3	broken	9
afraid	12	broken down	9
after a while	3	brunch	4
afternoon	1	buckle (noun & verb)	8
ages ago	2	buffet	4
all right	10	burned	6
aluminum	7	burst	9
angry	12	button (noun & verb)	8
annoyed	12	cable	8
anxious	12	café	4
around	3	cafeteria	4
at a later time	3	calm	12
at once	3	cardboard	7
at one time	2	careful	11
at present	2	careless	11
at the present time	2	caring	11
at this moment	2	cement	7
at this point	2	century	1
at this time	2	chew	5
attach	8	chip	9
attractive	10	chubby	10
awful	10	clay	7
bake	6	clever	11
banquet	4	clip (noun & verb)	8
bar	4	cloth	7
barbecue	4,6	coffee shop	4
beautiful	10	cold-hearted	11
before long	3	come apart	9
bite into	5	concerned	12
boil	6	concrete	7
bothered	12	connect	8
break	9	considerate	11
break into pieces	9	cook	6
break off	9	cooked	6
breakfast	4	cookout	4
brick	7	copper	7

cord	8	finish off	5
cotton	7	foolish	11
crack	9	friendly	11
crush	9	frightened	12
currently	2	fry	6
cute	10	fur	7
dawn	1	furious	12
day	1	generous	11
daybreak	1	gifted	11
decade	1	giving	11
deceitful	11	glass	7
deep-fry	6	glue *(noun & verb)*	8
dense	11	good	10
destroyed	9	good-hearted	11
digest	5	good-looking	10
dinner	4	gorgeous	10
dirt	7	great	10
dishonest	11	greedy	11
disloyal	11	grill	6
dizzy	10	grotesque	10
done	6	gulp down	5
drink	5	handsome	10
dumb	11	hard-hearted	11
dusk	1	heartless	11
early	3	heavy	10
earth	7	helpful	11
easy-going	12	hideous	10
eat	5	homely	10
eat like a bird	5	honest	11
eat like a pig	5	horrified	12
eat up	5	hot-dog stand	4
enraged	12	hour	1
evening	1	ideal weight	10
eventually	3	immediately	3
fabric	7	impolite	11
faint	10	in a little while	3
faithful	11	in a while	3
fall apart	9	in this day and age	2
fall to pieces	9	inconsiderate	11
fasten	8	insensitive	11
fast-food restaurant	4	intelligent	11
fat	10	iron	7
fearful	12	irresponsible	11
feverish	10	irritated	12
fine	10	join	8

kind	11	nowadays	2
kind-hearted	11	nylon	7
last month	2	obese	10
last night	2	okay	10
last week	2	on the blink	9
last year	2	on the dot	3
late	3	on time	3
later	3	one of these days	3
leather	7	out of order	9
lick	5	overdue	3
line	8	overeat	5
lovely	10	overweight	10
loyal	11	paper	7
lunch	4	paper clip	8
mad	12	paste (noun & verb)	8
masking tape	8	pebble	7
material	7	petrified	12
matter	7	pick at	5
meal	4	picnic	4
mean	11	pig out (on)	5
medium	6	pin	8
metal	7	plain	10
microwave	6	plastic	7
midnight	1	plump	10
minute	1	polish off	5
month	1	polite	11
morning	1	polyester	7
mud	7	potluck	4
munch on	5	pretty	10
nail (noun & verb)	8	pretty good	10
nasty	11	prompt	3
nauseous	10	pudgy	10
nervous	12	punctual	3
next month	2	put away	5
next week	2	put together	8
next year	2	quick	11
nibble on	5	rare	6
nice	11	ravishing	10
night	1	raw	6
noon	1	rayon	7
not bad	10	recently	2
not so good	10	refreshment stand	4
not so hot	10	relaxed	12
not working	9	reliable	11
now	2	responsible	11

restaurant	4	sometime	3
ribbon	8	sometime ago	2
right away	3	sometime soon	3
right now	2	soon	3
roast	6	sooner or later	3
rock	7	so-so	10
rope	8	staple	8
rotten	10	steam	6
rubber	7	steel	7
rubber cement	8	stew	6
rude	11	stingy	11
ruined	9	stir-fry	6
rupture	9	stone	7
safety pin	8	straight pin	8
sand	7	strap (noun & verb)	8
scared	12	string	8
scared stiff	12	stuff one's face (with)	5
scrawny	10	stupid	11
screw (noun & verb)	8	substance	7
second	1	suck on	5
sensitive	11	sundown	1
sharp	3, 11	sunrise	1
shatter	9	sunset	1
shortly	3	supper	4
sick	10	swallow	5
sick as a dog	10	tack (noun & verb)	8
sick to one's stomach	10	take a bite (of)	5
silk	7	tape (noun & verb)	8
simmer	6	tardy	3
sip	5	tense	12
skinny	10	terrified	12
slender	10	the day after tomorrow	2
slight	10	the day before yesterday	2
slim	10	the other day	2
slow	11	these days	2
slurp	5	thick	11
smart	11	thin	10
smash	9	this afternoon	2
snack	4	this evening	2
snack bar	4	this minute	3
snack machine	4	this month	2
snap (noun & verb)	8	this morning	2
soft-hearted	11	this week	2
soil	7	this year	2
someday	3	thoughtful	11

thoughtless	11	unreliable	11
tie	8	upset	12
toast	6	velcro	8
today	2	vending machine	4
tomorrow	2	very fat	10
tomorrow afternoon	2	very sick	10
tomorrow evening	2	very smart	11
tomorrow morning	2	very thin	10
tomorrow night	2	warm-hearted	11
tonight	2	week	1
totalled	9	well-done	6
truthful	11	wise	11
twilight	1	wood	7
ugly	10	wool	7
ultimately	3	worried	12
unattractive	10	wrecked	9
uncaring	11	year	1
uncooked	6	years ago	2
under the weather	10	yesterday	2
underweight	10	yesterday afternoon	2
unfaithful	11	yesterday evening	2
unfriendly	11	yesterday morning	2
unhelpful	11	zip	8
unintelligent	11	zipper	8
unkind	11		